F4F WILDCAT

MW00844781

in action

By Don Linn

Color By Don Greer
Illustrated By Perry Manley

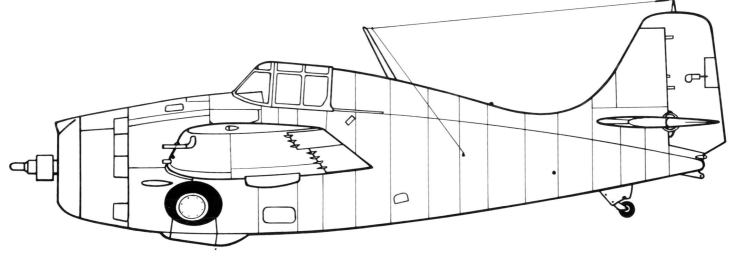

Aircraft Number 84
squadron/signal publications, inc.

LCDR John S Thatch leads a division of F4F-3 Wildcats of VF-3 aboard USS LEXINGTON in a combat air patrol above the task force on 1 February 1942. LEXINGTON was repeatedly attacked by Japanese bombers flying from Rabaul and owed her survival to the pilots and Wildcats of her fighter squadron, VF-3.

ISBN 0-89747-200-4

If you have any photographs of the aircraft, armor, soldiers or ships of any nation, particularly wartime snapshots, why not share them with us and help make Squadron/Signal's books all the more interesting and complete in the future. Any photograph sent to us will be copied and the original returned. The donor will be fully credited for any photos used. Please send them to:

Squadron/Signal Publications, Inc.
1115 Crowley Drive.
Carrollton, TX 75011-5010.

Acknowledgements

I wish to extend a special thank you to David W. Lucabaugh for the loan of a great number of Wildcat photographs from his personal collection. Dave's unselfish loan saved me many hours of research through the National Archives files and without his help I might not have been able to complete this book. Additionally, I wish to thank Robert F. Dorr for researching and obtaining photography from the Imperial War Museum in London. Another special thank you goes to CDR. Dennis White, OBE, FMA, RN (Retired) Director of the Fleet Air Arm Museum for the loan of his personal photographs and making photography from the Fleet Air Arm Museum available to me. And to Jim Dresser for suggesting useful photographic subjects from the National Archives. To each, a heartfelt thank you!

The following individuals all contributed their time, help, and encouragement in this project. Each deserves his own special thank you!

Don Spering/AIR	Stan Piet
Brian Pickering	Jim Sullivan
Ray Sturtviant	Dave Ostrowski
Ed Ireland	David F. Brown
Steve VanDerryt	Henry Singer
K. Yaffe/National Archives	Grumman Aerospace
Paul White/National Archives	Dana Bell/NASM
Donald Kirkpatrick	AAHS

This pair of F4F-3 Wildcats of VF-3 aboard USS LEXINGTON (CV-2) were flown by two of the Navy's early aces, LCDR John S. Thatch (F-1) and LT Edward 'Butch' O'Hare (F-13). LCDR Thatch finished the war with six and a half kills, while LT O'Hare was credited with seven enemy aircraft before he was killed in action on 24 November 1943. (National Archives)

INTRODUCTION

In 1935 the US Navy Bureau of Aeronautics issued a request for proposals to the US aviation industry for a new fighter design to replace the Grumman F3F. A number of designs were submitted and from these the Navy selected two for further development. In the Spring of 1936 the Navy awarded contracts for two prototype fighters, the Brewster XF2A-1 and the Grumman XF4F-1. Brewster's XF2A-1 prototype was a monoplane, while the Grumman design, the XF4F-1, was a biplane, similar to Grumman's earlier F3F-3 already in service. Grumman, realizing that its competitive edge could be lost if they continued with biplane designs while others were building monoplanes, sought the Navy's permission to change the XF4F-1 prototype from a biplane to a monoplane configuration. On 10 July 1936, the Navy agreed to the Grumman proposal. The XF4F-1 contract was cancelled and Grumman received authorization to build a prototype of the monoplane XF4F-2 in its place. The Grumman and Brewster prototypes would be flown in a competitive fly-off which would determine which design would receive a production contract.

XF4F-2 Prototype

With the cancellation of the XF4F-1 prototype, Grumman immediately began work on the XF4F-2 prototype. The sole XF4F-2 (BuNo 0383) prototype was an all metal mid-wing monoplane powered by a 1,050 hp Pratt & Whitney R-1830-66 engine turning a Hamilton Standard three blade propeller. The prototype bore a strong family resemblance to Grumman's earlier biplane fighters with the landing gear, fuselage, cockpit, and tail being similar to the earlier F3F-3 biplane. Armament consisted of two synchronized .30 caliber machine guns installed in the upper cowling firing through the propeller arc and provision for a .50 caliber machine gun in each wing. The main landing gear retracted into wells in the fuselage sides under the wing leading edge. The landing gear was raised and lowered by means of a hand crank (twenty-nine turns were required to fully retract or extend the landing gear) in the cockpit. The non-retractable fully swiveling tail wheel was mounted in a fairing under the rear fuselage even with the stabilizer leading edge. The rear sliding cockpit canopy was faired into the fuselage with a long graceful turtle deck. Two pairs of windows were installed in the lower fuselage below the wing to give the pilot a degree of downward vision. A fully retractable arresting hook was installed at the extreme end of the fuselage.

The prototype made its first flight on 2 September 1937 and began a three month series of factory trials. After completion of these tests Grumman delivered the prototype to Naval Air Station Anacostia, outside Washington, DC on 23 December 1937. The Navy immediately began its series of tests, including gunnery trials at Dahlgren, Virginia. These trials showed the XF4F-2 had a great deal of promise, with a demonstrated top speed of over 290 mph, however persistent problems with engine over heating plagued the tests. On 14 February 1938 the XF4F-2 was returned to Grumman so that Grumman engineers could correct the engine over heating problem. Various propellers, with and without spinners were tried and the cowling was modified with a blunter profile. Two days later Grumman test pilot Robert Hall flew the modified XF4F-2 to the Navy's Dahlgren Proving Grounds for final inspection trials. The prototype successfully completed these trials, however, the design competition fly-off still had to be won.

The design competition fly-off was held on 1 March 1938 at NAS Anacostia. Besides the XF4F-2 and XF2A-1, a third prototype the Seversky XNF-1 (a navalized version of the US Army Air Corps P-35), was entered in the competition. The initial flight trials between the three competitors were successful to some degree for each. The XF4F-2 had demonstrated the highest speed, however, when deck handling and catapult trials were begun on 6 April at the Naval Aircraft Factory in Philadelphia, problems with engine over heating again surfaced.

The XF4F-2 prototype (BuNo 0383) on the Grumman ramp at Bethpage. The prototype flew on 2 September 1937 entering competition with the Brewster XF2A-1 and Seversky XNF-1 for the Navy's first monoplane fighter contract. Persistent engine problems with the XF4F-2 led the Navy to declare Brewster the winner of the competition. (Grumman)

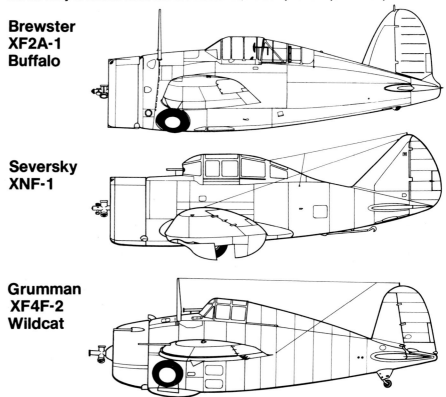

Brewster XF2A-1 Buffalo

Seversky XNF-1

Grumman XF4F-2 Wildcat

During deck handling trials at the Philadelphia Navy Yard the XF4F-2 crashed after suffering an engine failure. The prototype was rebuilt with a Pratt & Whitney XR-1830-76 engine under the designation XF4F-3. The XF4F-3 featured longer span wings with angular wing tips and redesigned tail surfaces with straight leading edges and a raked rudder. (Grumman)

In an effort to improve engine cooling Grumman tried a number of different propellers, propeller spinners, and cowl flap arrangements. This large propeller spinner was found to be ineffective and was not used on production F4F-3s. (Grumman)

Navy test pilot LT Gurney was conducting a test flight when he experienced a complete engine failure in the XF4F-2. LT Gurney managed to make a dead stick landing in a field on the Campbell Soup Company farm, just across the Delaware River from the Naval Aircraft Factory. On landing the gear dug into the soft earth and the prototype flipped over onto its back. Gurney emerged from the wreck shaken, bruised, but otherwise unhurt. The XF4F-2 was was not so fortunate, it was badly damaged and had to be returned to Bethpage for extensive repairs. Because of the persistent engine problems with the XF4F-2 the Navy selected the Brewster XF2A-1 as the winner of the competition and in June of 1938 awarded a production contract to Brewster for fifty-four fighters under the designation F2A-1.

In its final report the Navy review panel considered the Seversky XNF-1 to be totally impractical for the Navy's needs, however, the board felt the XF4F-2 warranted further development. Grumman engineers set about redesigning the XF4F-2 to accept an experimental Pratt & Whitney supercharged engine that would give 1,200 horsepower for takeoff and 1,000 horsepower at altitude. In October of 1938 Grumman received a Navy contract to convert the damaged XF4F-2 prototype to accept the Pratt & Whitney engine under the designation XF4F-3.

XF4F-3

The Grumman engineering team began work on modifying the existing, although badly damaged, XF4F-2 airframe to mount the prototype two stage two speed supercharged 1,200 hp Pratt & Whitney XR-1830-76 Twin Wasp engine. The fuselage was rebuilt and reinforced and the cowling was enlarged. To compensate for the added weight of the new engine, the wing was redesigned increasing both span and chord. The rounded wingtips were squared off and an oil cooler intake was mounted under the inboard wing panels. The tail surfaces were changed from the original rounded leading edge and rudder to a straight leading edge and raked rudder. The antenna mast on the port side of the fuselage in front of the cockpit was changed from a straight mast to a forward raked mast. The landing gear, cockpit and center fuselage sections were unchanged from the original XF4F-2 airframe.

In January of 1939 a production version of the 1,200 hp Pratt & Whitney R-1830 Twin Wasp engine was installed and, following ground engine tests, the XF4F-3 made its first

flight on 12 February 1939. Shortly afterward the prototype was flown to NAS Anacostia for Navy flight testing.

At Anacostia the XF4F-3 reached a top speed of 334 mph at 20,000 feet, rate of climb was 2,800 feet per minute and the service ceiling was 35,000 feet. Performance of the XF4F-3 was superior to the production Brewster F2A-1 in all respects. In order to improve engine cooling a number of modifications and improvements were made to the cowling and various propeller/spinner combinations were tested. In the event, a Curtiss Electric cuffed three blade propeller was installed which increased cooling airflow to the engine, solving the engine cooling problem.

While these changes were being made to the engine installation, other changes were made to the fuselage to improve the prototype's aerodynamics. The shape of the fin was changed with the fin leading edge faired into the upper fuselage and the rake of the rudder was reduced. The bottom of the rudder was angled to provide clearance for the retractable tail hook and the tailplane was repositioned from the fuselage to a position low on the fin. The radio antenna mast was moved from in front of the cockpit to a position on the fuselage spine behind the cockpit. In August of 1939, after four years of design and development work, The Navy was satisfied with the XF4F-3 and Grumman was awarded a production contract for fifty-four aircraft under the designation F4F-3.

The XF4F-3 went through a number of changes to improve the prototype's aerodynamics and engine cooling. In its final form the prototype had the horizontal stabilizers moved to a position low on the fin, the leading edge of the fin was faired into the fuselage spine, and the radio mast was moved from in front of the cockpit to the fuselage spine behind the cockpit. (Grumman)

Development

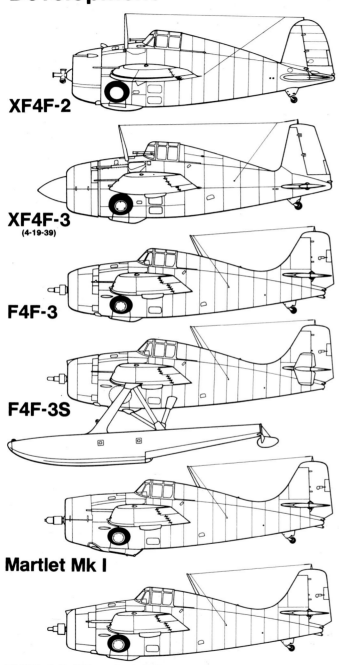

XF4F-2

XF4F-3
(4-19-39)

F4F-3

F4F-3S

Martlet Mk I

F4F-3A/Martlet Mk III

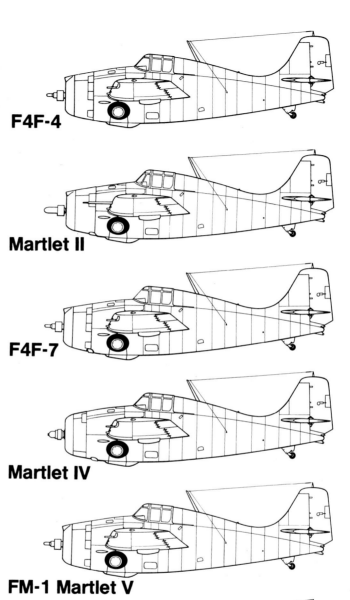

F4F-4

Martlet II

F4F-7

Martlet IV

FM-1 Martlet V

FM-2/Wildcat VI

F4F-3

The first F4F-3 off the Grumman assembly line was completed in January of 1940. This pre-production aircraft was delivered to the Naval Aircraft Factory at Philadelphia for static testing. The first production F4F-3 Wildcat (BuNo 1844) made its first flight during February of 1940 and immediately entered a series of factory tests. The flight tests revealed that the unpressurized fuel system of the F4F-3 allowed fuel to boil at high altitudes causing the engine to run rough. To correct the problem the first production aircraft (BuNo 1844) was modified to incorporate a fuel pressurization system consisting of a rubber fuel bladder installed inside the 130 gallon main fuselage fuel tank. The pressurized fuel system eliminated engine roughness at high altitudes, however, the fuel bladder reduced the capacity of the fuselage fuel tank by thirteen gallons.

In August of 1940 BuNo 1844 was flown to the Pratt & Whitney engine factory to serve as a test bed for further engine development. The second production aircraft (BuNo 1845) flew in July of 1940 and was delivered to NAS Anacostia the following month for Navy Production Inspection Trials.

The first two production aircraft carried an armament of two .30 caliber machine guns mounted in the upper fuselage decking and two .50 caliber machine guns mounted in the wings. Reports of aerial combat in Europe quickly convinced Navy officials that this armament was inadequate and a change was ordered for all subsequent production F4F-3s. The two upper fuselage mounted .30 caliber guns were deleted and two additional .50 caliber machine guns with 450 rounds of ammunition per gun were installed in each wing. The guns were staggered with the blast tubes of the two inboard guns extending ahead of the wing leading edge.

The Navy was concerned that Pratt & Whitney might not be able to successfully complete development of the two stage supercharged R-1830-76 engine and ordered the third and fourth production aircraft (BuNos 1846 and 1847) modified to accept the 1,200 hp Wright R-1820-40 engine under the experimental designation XF4F-5. The fifth and sixth production aircraft (BuNos 1848 and 1851) were completed with the four wing gun armament, strengthened landing gear and armor protection for the pilot.

These early production F4F-3s were subjected to an extensive series of Navy tests and evaluations. During November of 1940 they were joined by another experimental prototype, the XF4F-6. The XF4F-6 was a standard production F4F-3 modified with a 1,200 hp single stage supercharged Pratt & Whitney R-1830-90 engine replacing the two stage supercharged R-1830-76. The Navy had ordered this installation as a trial aircraft to evaluate the lower rated engine and as a precaution against possible failure in the development of the two stage supercharged R-1830-76.

By the end of 1940 the Navy had completed its evaluation of the F4F-3. The trials board report recommended acceptance of the F4F-3 with minor modifications to the cockpit layout, addition of a strengthened tail wheel, and improved engine cooling. BuNo 1485 was flown to the National Advisory Committee for Aeronautics (NACA) Langley Field facility for a series of tests aimed at improving engine cooling. Various combinations of cuffed propellers and cowl flaps were tried until a final configuration of a cuffed Curtiss Electric propeller and double wide cowl flaps was found to solve the engine heating problem. This configuration became standard on all early production F4F-3s.

With the expansion of naval air power authorized by Congress during the summer of 1940, production contracts for the F4F-3 were increased dramatically. The original production contract for fifty-four aircraft was raised to over 200 F4F-3s. Production accelerated slowly, however, by 31 December 1940 twenty-two F4F-3s had been accepted by the Navy and were in squadron service.

The first Navy fleet squadrons to receive the F4F-3 were VF-7 attached to USS WASP and VF-4 embarked on USS RANGER. These early F4F-3s were delivered in the standard Navy pre-war color scheme, with an Aluminum painted fuselage and Chrome

The full White cowl ring band identified this F4F-3 of VF-42 as being assigned to the squadron's second section leader. The small national insignia on the nose was adopted in March of 1940 for carrier aircraft operating in the Atlantic on Neutrality Patrol. Wildcats carried the colorful pre-war markings for only a short period, from December of 1940 to March of 1941. (National Archives/D. Lucabaugh)

Yellow upper wing surfaces. F4F-3s going to VF-4 had the tail surfaces painted Willow Green, the assigned color of USS RANGER's air wing, while those assigned to VF-7 had their tails painted Black, USS WASP's air wing color. Both squadrons were deployed aboard their respective carriers during January of 1941 for a training cruise to Cuba. This cruise marked the first operational deployment of the World's first shipboard fighter equipped with a two stage supercharged engine.

The deployment also revealed several problems with the F4F-3 that had gone undetected during the service tests. The F4F-3 was fitted with a pair of emergency flotation bags installed in the outer wing panels. The flotation bags were designed to keep the aircraft afloat long enough for the pilot to escape in the event of a water landing. On several occasions during the 1941 training cruise the bags inflated during flight, usually during a high speed dive. At least two F4F-3s were lost from crashes that resulted when the inflated bags threw the F4Fs into an uncontrollable spin. To cure the problem, the Navy ordered the flotation bags removed from the F4F's wings. After a series of windshield failures during high speed dives, the Navy ordered the lower windshield panels replaced with stronger plexiglass panels.

The seventh F4F-3 off the Grumman assemble line was painted in the markings of VF-41 aboard USS RANGER with an Aluminum painted fuselage, Lemon Yellow upper wing surfaces and Willow Green tail surfaces. The cowl ring, fuselage band, and wing chevrons are White, outlined in Black. (National Archives/D. Lucabaugh)

An early production F4F-3 of VF-72 crash landed at Guantanamo Bay, Cuba on 25 February 1941. The tail surfaces are Gloss Black, the identification color of USS WASP, while the cowl band and wing chevrons are Gloss Black outlined in White. VF-72 carried the Neutrality star on the cowling of its F4F-3s. (National Archives/D. Lucabaugh)

The cockpit of an F4F-3. The main instrument panel had the flight instruments grouped together on the center console with engine instruments located on the two side panels. (Grumman)

Armament Development

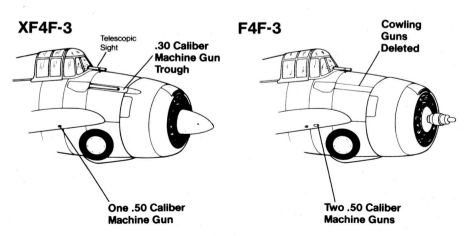

XF4F-3

Telescopic Sight

.30 Caliber Machine Gun Trough

One .50 Caliber Machine Gun

F4F-3

Cowling Guns Deleted

Two .50 Caliber Machine Guns

The main electrical control box is mounted above the landing gear retraction handle on the starboard side of the cockpit. To raise or lower the landing gear the gear handle had to be turned twenty-nine revolutions. (Grumman)

The port side of the F4F-3 cockpit had the trim tab controls (elevator, rudder and aileron) grouped behind and above the throttle. The silver handle located at the top right side of the cockpit is the tail hook control handle. (Grumman)

The training cruise revealed another problem with the F4F-3, although this problem would remain throughout the F4F's career. Pilots quickly became dissatisfied with the manual landing gear retraction system. On takeoff it took twenty-nine turns of the hand crank to completely retract the landing gear; at a time when the pilot was busy trying to hold a climb, join with his section and trim the aircraft. Lowering the landing gear down was equally difficult. If the pilot lowered the landing gear at too high an airspeed, or lost his grip on the handle, the retraction handle would being spinning rapidly. This led to a number of sprained wrists and incidents of jammed landing gear.

Twenty-one new production F4F-3s, with protective engine covers, are parked in a field near the Bethpage runway awaiting delivery to their new owners, Marine Fighter Squadron (VMF) 121. The Wildcats are camouflaged overall Light Gray with White fuselage codes. (Grumman)

F4F-3A

In late 1940 the Navy was concerned that possible delays in production of the two stage supercharged Pratt & Whitney R-1830-86 engine might slow deliveries of F4F-3s. As a precaution the Navy placed an order for ninety-five production versions of the XF4F-6 prototype under the designation F4F-3A. The F4F-3A was identical to the F4F-3 except for the engine. A 1,200 hp single stage, two speed supercharged Pratt and Whitney R-1830-90 engine was installed in place of the two stage, two speed R-1830-86. The cowling was identical to the early F4F-3 with the lip carburetor air scoop and double wide cowl flaps.

Pilots reported that the handling characteristics of the F4F-3A were not as good as the F4F-3. The single stage, two speed supercharger caused a loss of power at altitude when compared to the F4F-3. Top speed was reduced from 331 mph at 21,000 feet (F4F-3) to 312 mph for the F4F-3A.

F4F-3As were interspersed on the same production line as the F4F-3 and were delivered between March and May of 1941. Early in the production run the Navy agreed to divert thirty of the ninety-five F4F-3As for delivery to the Greek Navy. In the event these aircraft were never delivered to Greece. The aircraft were still at sea when Greece fell and were eventually taken over by the British.

F4F-3 (Late Production)

Pratt & Whitney had continued development of the -76 engine and now offered a version with improved reliability. After Grumman had produced 100 F4F-3s with the Pratt & Whitney R-1830-76 engine, the Navy ordered a switch to the -86 engine. The R-1830-86 featured a revised magneto layout and carburetor intake. The cowling of the F4F-3 was modified to accept the new engine with the lip carburetor air intake being replaced by an intake mounted inside the cowling. The cowl flaps were changed from a single double wide flap on each side of the cowling to eight cowl flaps, three mounted together high on each side of the cowling and two installed just above the exhaust stack on each side of the cowling. The Navy felt the engine change did not warrant a model number designator change and retained the F4F-3 designation for the revised -86 powered aircraft.

In October of 1941 the Navy began assigning names as well as designations to fleet aircraft and the F4F was officially assigned the name Wildcat. As the fleet squadrons began working up with their new mounts, the telescopic gun sight, mounted in the windshield center section was replaced by a modern reflector gun sight. To protect the pilot, an armor glass panel was also installed immediately behind the windshield. By the time of the Japanese attack on Pearl Harbor on 7 December 1941, the Navy had taken delivery of 187 F4F-3s and fifty-eight F4F-3As. Eight first line Navy and three Marine Corps fighter squadrons were equipped with Wildcats and others were in training.

The first Wildcats to see combat where twelve F4F-3s of Marine Fighter Squadron 211 (VMF 211) which made up the air defense of Wake Island. On 8 December 1941 a four plane CAP was airborne but because of bad weather missed intercepting the first Japanese raid. Thirty-six Mitsubishi G3M medium bombers attacked the island under the cover of low clouds and rain, hitting the runways, maintenance area, and flight line. Seven of the eight Wildcats on the flight line were destroyed, reducing Wake's air defense to five Wildcats.

Throughout the next two weeks the Marines kept the Wildcats flying by cannibalizing wrecked aircraft, improvising tools, and hand making some parts. When the Japanese attempted their first landings on Wake early on the morning of 11 December, four Wildcats attacked the invasion fleet with 100 pound bombs and .50 caliber machine gun fire. During the fighting the Japanese destroyer *Kisaragi* was sunk and a number of other ships were damaged by the Wildcats, forcing the Japanese invasion force to retire.

The first production F4F-3A (BuNo 3905) on the Grumman ramp on 7 April 1941. The F3F-3A was powered by a 1,200 hp Pratt & Whitney R-1830-90 engine in place of the R-1830-76 of the F4F-3. Thirty F4F-3As were diverted from the Navy contract for delivery to Greece, however, these aircraft were still at sea when Greece fell and were diverted to Gibralter. (Grumman)

A late production F4F-3 of VF-3 rides the elevator to the flight deck of USS SARATOGA (CV-3) during the Spring of 1941. Late production F4F-3s were powered by 1,200 hp Pratt & Whitney R-1830-86 engines and featured a modified cowling. The lip air intake was deleted and four cowl flaps have been added to each side of the cowl, replacing the earlier double wide flaps. (National Archives/D. Lucabaugh)

Eleven days later the Japanese returned, reinforced by carrier aircraft, for the final assault on Wake. The remaining two Wildcats attacked a thirty-nine aircraft raid from the Japanese carriers *Soryu* and *Hiryu*. One was quickly shot down by escorting A6M Zero fighters, but the second Wildcat shot down two of the raiders before the pilot, CAPT Herb Frueler, was wounded. Frueler managed to return to the island where he crash landed, wrecking Wake's last Wildcat. The island fell to the Japanese on 23 December 1941.

To make the F4F-3 a more combat capable fighter the Navy ordered a number of field modifications. On 11 December 1941 a BUAIR change order was issued instructing that self-sealing fuel tanks and armor be installed on all F4F-3 and F4F-3A aircraft. A 126 gallon self-sealing bladder type fuel tank was installed in the fuselage replacing the 117 gallon main fuselage fuel tank. These early self sealing tanks, however, had a tendency to shed rubber which clogged the fuel system and a number of Wildcats were lost when their engines failed from fuel starvation.

Navy pilots soon began reporting that the Wildcat's four Browning .50 caliber machine guns jammed in combat for no apparent reason. During flight trials and training before the war, the Brownings had operated perfectly, however, under combat conditions the guns suffered frequent jamming.

Navy ordnancemen of Fighter Squadron Six (VF-6) operating from USS ENTER-PRISE investigated the gun jams and found the problem lay in the ammunition feed trays. They found that a full load of belted .50 caliber ammunition would shift in the ammunition trays during violent combat maneuvers causing the guns to misfeed and jam. The problem had not surfaced before because, during testing and training, the F4Fs had not been flown with full ammunition loads. Their report was forwarded to the Bureau of Aeronautics, which had already received similar reports from Wildcat squadrons operating in the Atlantic.

In their report, ENTERPRISE and VF-6 ordnancemen had suggested a possible fix for the problem. Their idea was to install dividers in the ammunition magazine trays to prevent the ammunition belts from shifting and jamming the guns. The Bureau of Aeronautics tested the idea and found it solved the problem. A message was issued on 11 March 1942 with instructions for modifying the trays with dividers, curing the jamming problem.

Cowling

F4F-3 (Early)
(P&W R-1830-76 Engine)

F4F-3 (Late)
(P&W R-1830-86 Engine)

F4F-3A
(P&W R-1830-90 Engine)

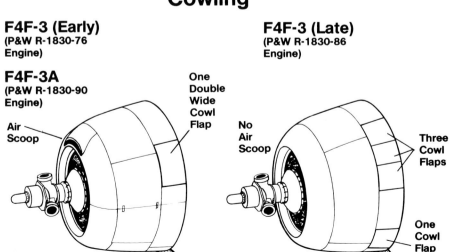

Air Scoop
One Double Wide Cowl Flap

No Air Scoop
Three Cowl Flaps
One Cowl Flap

Navy aviation machinist mates work on an F4F-3 of VF-3 on the hanger deck of USS ENTERPRISE (CV-6). Douglas SBDs and TBDs with their wings removed are suspended from overhead beams to provide additional working space on the hanger deck. The "Felix the Cat" squadron insignia of VF-3 is painted just below the Wildcat's windscreen. (National Archives/D. Lucabaugh)

VF-3 maintenance crews work on a late production F4F-3 Wildcat on the hanger deck of USS ENTERPRISE (CV-6). A variety of spare propellers for the ship's airwing are suspended from an overhead beam behind the Wildcat. Space was always at a premium aboard carriers and little was wasted. (National Archives)

11

An F4F-3 of VF-41 armed with 100 pound bombs taxies forward aboard USS RANGER (CV-4) in December of 1941. The individual aircraft number "14" is repeated in White on each wing leading edge. The small square above the bomb on the port wing is the window for the internal gun camera. (National Archives/D. Lucabaugh)

F4F-3P

At least ten F4F-3 fighters were converted to armed photo reconnaissance aircraft under the designation F4F-3P. The conversion consisted of a 30 inch focal length aerial camera installed in the lower starboard fuselage with a pulley operated trap door covering the camera opening. All F4F-3Ps were field conversions performed by Navy repair depots. The camera installation was not standardized and varied from aircraft to aircraft. A number of F4F-3Ps were assigned to Marine Observation Squadron (VMO) 251 and saw service at Espiritu in the New Hebrides during 1943, while at least two others were used during the invasion of North Africa by Fighter Squadron 41 (VF-41). Known F3F-3P conversions are BuNos 1849, 1852, 1856, 1865, 1867, 1870, 1871, 1875, 1880, and 1894.

This F4F-3 has an unusual mix of markings. The Wildcat carries the Red and White rudder stripes first introduced on 5 January 1942 but retains the fuselage code in White instead of Flat Black as was specified for Intermediate Blue Gray over Light Gray camouflaged F4Fs four months earlier in October of 1941. (Grumman)

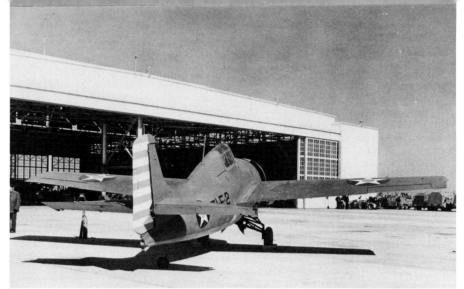

An F4F-3 of VF-71 assigned to USS WASP (CV-7) runs up its engine at Naval Air Station Norfolk, Virginia on 10 February 1942. The small round object at the base of the rudder is the White tail position light, the retractable tail hook is below it, and the bracket on the underside of the tail is the aircraft towing lug. (National Archives/D. Lucabaugh)

Gunsights

F4F-3 (Early)
Telescopic Gunsight

F4F-3/3A (Late)
Deflector Gunsight

Armor Glass Panel

The flight deck officer gives the launch signal to an F4F-3 of VF-3 aboard USS ENTERPRISE (CV-6) during early 1942. The Wildcat is armed with a 100 pound bomb on the starboard wing bomb rack while the port bomb rack is empty. (National Archives)

An F4F-3 of VF-8 on patrol during early 1942. The Flat Black code on the fuselage side, '8-F-1', identifies the squadron, squadron type (F for fighter) and individual aircraft within the squadron. (AAHS)

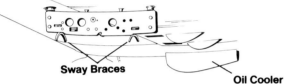

Bomb Rack
(Optional)

Sway Braces

Oil Cooler

As the war progressed so did the changes in markings and national insignia. This VF-3 Wildcat is being painted with the enlarged national insignia ordered by the Navy on 5 January 1942. (National Archives)

The flight deck of USS ENTERPRISE (CV-6) is crowded with F4F-3s of VF-6 as plane captains and armorers work on the aircraft. Only two of the Wildcats have the Red and White rudder stripes (F-7 and F-18) painted correctly. The remainder are non-standard with five Red stripes instead of seven. (National Archives/D. Lucabaugh)

13

LT Edward 'Butch' O'Hare in the cockpit of his F4F-3 of VF-3 on 10 April 1942. LT O'Hare was awarded the Congressional Medal of Honor for shooting down five Japanese bombers and saving the USS LEXINGTON (CV-2) from attack. (National Archives/D. Lucabaugh)

An F4F-3A of VF-6 aboard USS ENTERPRISE (CV-6) prepares to deck launch during the Marcus Island raid of 25 March 1942. The broad angular wing of the Wildcat blocked the pilots downward vision, and while the two small windows on the lower fuselage provided a limited downward view, in combat Wildcat pilots quickly developed a habit of dipping the wings to see what was below them. (National Archives/D. Lucabaugh)

A section of F4F-3 Wildcats of VF-2 prepares to launch from USS ENTERPRISE (CV-6) for a combat air patrol on 12 May 1942. One of the primary identification features of the F4F-3 is the protruding barrel of the inboard .50 caliber machine gun. (National Archives/D. Lucabaugh)

An F4F-3 on a combat air patrol during late 1942. The two antennas under the center of the fuselage are aerials for the ZB-3 navigational radio receiver and AN/ARR-2 radio receiver. (Grumman)

14

(Above) This F4F-3 carries a 35mm gun camera mounted on the starboard wing root for gunnery training. The odd shaped port wing national insignia was caused by a wing panel being replaced with a spare from a Wildcat with a different style wing insignia. (Grumman)

(Below) A makeshift hangar was erected on Espiritu Santo by the Marines of VMO-251 to shield them from the hot sun and tropical rains while working on their photo reconnaissance Wildcats. This F4F-3P has a camera mounted in the lower starboard side of the fuselage with a pulley operated trap door covering the camera window. (National Archives/D. Lucabaugh)

(Above) A Grumman test pilot demonstrates deployment of the internal life raft carried on the F4F-3. In service, however, Wildcats would often sink before the life raft could be released. Eventually a one man raft carried in the pilot's seat pack survival kit became standard.

F4F-3S *Wildcatfish*

The US Navy had been impressed with the success of the Japanese Nakajima A6M2-N Rufe float fighter during the early fighting in the Pacific. These floatplanes, operating from sheltered harbors, provided the Japanese with fighter cover in forward areas where no airfields existed.

The Navy considered the Wildcat a likely candidate for a similar conversion and in October of 1942 an F4F-3 (BuNo 4038) was sent to the Edo Corporation's Long Island plant to be fitted with floats. The Wildcat was fitted with a twin float installation attached to the wing and fuselage with long streamlined struts (unlike the Japanese Rufe which used a single main float and small outrigger wing floats) and the wheel wells faired over. To overcome yaw instability resulting from the large float area, small movable rudders were added to the tips of the horizontal stabilizers. The conversion was completed during mid-February of 1943 and the prototype made its first flight on 28 February with Grumman test pilot F. 'Hank' Kurt at the controls.

On 5 March the float Wildcat, named the *Wildcatfish*, was flown to NAS Anacostia for Navy trials. During these trials it was discovered that directional control was still unsatisfactory and the prototype was modified with a large ventral fin to improve yaw control. On 6 June the prototype was flown to NAS Norfolk for rough water trials. These tests proved the design to be satisfactory for water operation in wave heights up to two feet. The success of the sea trials led to plans to convert one hundred F4F-3s to the float configuration and Edo received orders for 100 sets of Wildcat floats.

The Wildcatfish, however, would never be used operationally for two equally important reasons. Navy trials showed that the float Wildcat had a top speed of 241 mph, almost a hundred miles an hour slower than a standard F4F-3. The drag imposed by the floats lowered the F4F's performance to the point that it would have been ineffective against any Japanese front line fighter. Additionally the need for float equipped fighters soon became unnecessary since the Navy's Seabees (Construction Battalions) had proven to be remarkably adept at quickly carving airfields out of island jungles and coral beaches . The speed at which the Seabees worked allowed deployment of shore based standard F4Fs to do the job the floatplane fighters were intended to do.

The Wildcatfish project was abandoned and the order for one hundred float equipped F4F-3s was cancelled and the F4F-3s already in production for the project were delivered to the Naval Air Training Command as standard wheel equipped F4F-3s during 1943.

The prototype F4F-3S Wildcatfish on the seaplane ramp at NAS Norfolk on 2 December 1942. The small wheels attached to the floats are beaching gear used for moving the aircraft on land and were removed before flight. The fins on the horizontal stabilizer are auxiliary rudders linked with the main rudder to improve the prototype's lateral stability. (Grumman)

Float Mounting

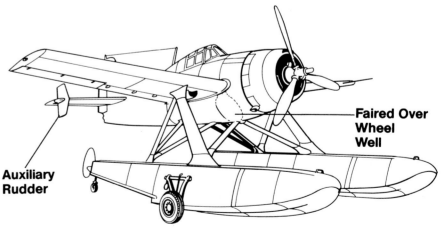

Faired Over Wheel Well

Auxiliary Rudder

(Left) The F4F-3S prototype during sea trials at NAS Norfolk, Virginia. The sea trials showed that the Wildcatfish could safely operate in wave heights up to two feet. Performance of the F4F-3S was disappointing and no production was undertaken. (Grumman)

Grumman G-36A/Martlet Mk I

The threat posed by the Axis Powers in Europe during the late 1930s led most European countries to begin programs aimed at improving and modernizing their air forces. Most European governments realized that national aircraft production would have to be supplemented by purchases from abroad. As a result various government buying commissions were sent to the United States in an effort to buy American military aircraft. France, England, and Greece each sent purchasing commissions to the United States and export variants of the F4F were among the aircraft considered by these commissions.

During late 1939 the French Purchasing Commission ordered eighty-one Wildcats under the Grumman export designation G-36A to equip their carrier based squadrons aboard the carrier BEARN and two other carriers then under construction, the JOFFERE and PAINLEVE. The G-36A was basically similar to the F4F-3, however, the French specified a number of changes.

Since the Pratt & Whitney fourteen cylinder R-1830-76 engine used in the F4F-3 was not cleared for export, the French G-36As were powered by a nine cylinder 1,200 hp Wright R-1820-G205A Cyclone engine driving a Hamilton Standard uncuffed propeller. The cowling of the G-36A was modified to accept the smaller Wright engine, having a narrower chord and no cowl flaps. Armament specified for the G-36A was four 7.65MM Darne machine guns mounted in the wings and two Darne machine guns mounted in the upper fuselage firing through the propeller arc. Armament was to be installed after delivery, however, French radio equipment and gunsights were furnished and were installed on the production line. The throttle linkage on the G-36A was reversed from standard American installations to correspond with the French system of throttle operation.

On 11 May 1940 the first G-36A lifted off on its maiden flight from the Bethpage runway, unfortunately the German army invaded France two days later and after production of seven G-36As the French order was cancelled.

The British Purchasing Commission had placed an order for 100 aircraft powered by 1,200 hp Pratt & Whitney S3C4-G engines under the Grumman export designation G-36B. The Commission, however, had learned of the folding wing XF4F-4 and had amended their contract to specify folding wings even though it would mean a delay in deliveries. When the French G-36A contract was canceled, the British offered to take over the contract and re-instate production of the G-36As under the British designation Martlet Mk I.

The first Martlet Mk Is were delivered on 27 July 1940 after being modified to British standards. The French armament was replaced by four wing mounted .50 caliber machine guns. The throttle operation was again reversed and British radios and gunsights replaced the French equipment. The first six Martlet Is were disassembled and shipped to England during August of 1940 where they were re-assembled by Scottish Aviation. One Martlet was sent to the British testing establishment at Boscombe Down with the remainder being assigned to Fleet Air Arm No 804 Squadron, based at Hatston.

It was two Martlets of this squadron that claimed the first combat victory gained by the Wildcat when they shot down a *Luftwaffe* Ju 88A on 25 December 1940, almost twelve months before US Marine F4F-3s entered combat over Wake. The German bomber had been on a reconnaissance mission over the British Home Fleet base at Scapa Flow. This important base in the Orkney Islands, just off the coast of Scotland in the North Sea, had been under observation by German reconnaissance aircraft for some time. Sea Gladiators of No 804 squadron had been unable to halt the intrusions, however, the Martlets had no difficulty in intercepting the intruder and shooting it down. To commemorate the event the squadron sent the propeller from one of the intercepting Martlet Is to Grumman.

The first G-36A Wildcat (export version of the F4F-3) for the French *Aeronaval*. France ordered eighty-one G-36As armed with two fuselage mounted and four wing mounted French made Darne 7.65MM machine guns. In the event none of the Wildcats were delivered to France and the contract was taken over by the British. (Grumman)

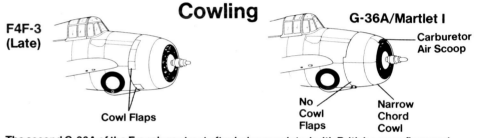

Cowling

F4F-3 (Late)

G-36A/Martlet I
— Carburetor Air Scoop

Cowl Flaps

No Cowl Flaps — Narrow Chord Cowl

The second G-36A of the French contract after being repainted with British camouflage and markings. The US civil registration NXG2 was a temporary marking carried on the wing in White during factory test flights. The British took delivery of the ex-French Wildcats under the designation Martlet Mk I. (Don Spering/AIR)

17

(Above) A Martlet Mk I (AL257) of either No 759 Squadron or No 778 Squadron Fleet Air Arm over England during June of 1940. The protruding barrels of the four wing mounted .50 caliber machine guns and narrow chord cowling are the primary identification features of the Martlet Mk I. (F.A.A. Museum)

(Below) This Martlet Mk I (AL246) is the only remaining Wildcat/Martlet of the hundreds that served with the Fleet Air Arm. The aircraft has been preserved and is on display in the Fleet Air Arm Museum at Yeovilton, England. (Grumman)

Wing Armament

F4F-3

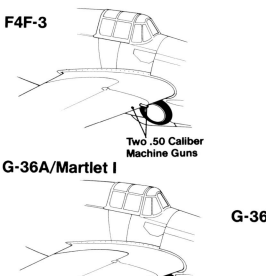

Two .50 Caliber
Machine Guns

G-36A/Martlet I

Two .50 Caliber
Machine Guns

Propellers

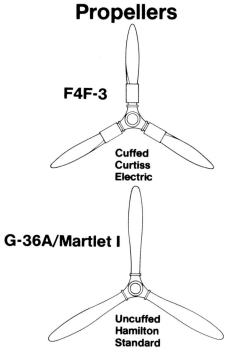

F4F-3

Cuffed
Curtiss
Electric

G-36A/Martlet I

Uncuffed
Hamilton
Standard

Martlet III

In June of 1940 Italy entered the Second World War on the side of Germany by declaring war on France and England, invading Greece four months later in October of 1940. The Greeks urgently requested assistance from both the Allies and the United States to resist the Italian invasion. Part of the assistance offered by the United States were thirty F4F-3As diverted from US Navy contracts and funded under the Lend Lease Act of 11 March 1941. The Greeks eagerly accepted the Wildcats and all thirty were enroute to Greece by the end of March.

The thirty F4F-3As were still at sea when German forces invaded Greece on 6 April 1941. The ship carrying the Wildcats was diverted to the British base at Gibraltar to await further orders. The overall Azure Blue Wildcats, bearing US Navy BuNos (assigned for contractual purposes) were turned over to British control at Gibraltar and assigned the British designation Martlet Mk III. After being repainted with British insignia, these aircraft were used to form Nos 805 and 806 Squadrons which operated from land bases as part of the Royal Navy Fighter Unit assigned to the Western Desert.

The British later assigned serial numbers AX725 - AX747 to the Martlet IIIs. The fixed wing Martlet IIIs primarily operated from land bases, their only known action at sea being when No 806 Squadron deployed aboard HMS INDOMITABLE for convoy escort duty in the Mediterranean. The convoy sailed from Gibralter bound for Malta in August of 1942. During the convoy escort mission the squadron lost three Martlets in action against claims of four German and Italian aircraft destroyed.

(Above) Martlet IIIs of No 805 Squadron return to their desert landing field in North Africa following a combat patrol. The Martlets have been camouflaged with Midstone uppersurfaces over Azure Blue undersurfaces. No 805 Squadron primarily used the Martlets for ground attacks against Italian and German installations. (F.A.A. Museum)

A Martlet Mk III of the Royal Navy Fighter Unit in the Western Desert during 1941. The US Navy BuNo (3676) has been retained and is painted in Black on the fuselage side below the horizontal stabilizer. (FAA)

19

F4F-4

During early 1938 the Navy recognized that the fixed thirty-eight foot wings of the F4F-3 would restrict the number of aircraft that could be carried on board aircraft carriers. In March of 1940, the Navy issued Grumman a contract to modify the last production F4F-3 (BuN0 1897) with folding wings under the designation XF4F-4.

Most carrier aircraft of the period folded the wings vertically, which saved space but caused some problem with overhead clearance when the aircraft were parked on the ship's hangar deck. Grumman devised a unique hydraulic wing fold system for the XF4F-4 that allowed the outer wing panels to pivot around the main spar and fold back along the fuselage sides. This eliminated the height problem and allowed a substantial reduction of the space needed to park the XF4F-4. With the wings folded the wingspan of the XF4F-4 was reduced from thirty-eight feet to fourteen feet four inches.

The cowling of the XF4F-4 was reconfigured with the carburetor air intake being repositioned outside the cowling on the upper lip of the cowl ring. The pitot tube was changed from a straight tube protruding from the port wing tip to a short "L" shaped tube mounted under the port wing tip.

Grumman also increased the armament of the XF4F-4, installing an additional .50 caliber machine gun in each wing. The six .50 caliber machine guns of the XF4F-4 carried 240 rounds per gun for a total of 1,440 rounds of ammunition, 360 rounds less than the F4F-3 (450 rounds per gun). Experienced Navy fighter pilots objected to the reduction in ammunition and many felt that they would have rather kept the four gun installation with its higher ammunition loads. The six gun installation was a compromise to facilitate simultaneous production of Wildcats ordered by the British (who specified a six gun wing) and Navy F4F-4s. In order to maintain production schedules the Navy agreed and the XF4F-4 was modified with a six gun installation. Lt John Adams of VF-42 later reported that...*The reduction in rounds per gun with the six .50 caliber machine guns cut the firing time by at least five seconds. That doesn't sound like much, but can be a lifetime in combat...*

The prototype first flew on 14 April 1941 and the Navy accepted delivery of the XF4F-4 in May of 1941. The prototype was assigned to VF-42 at NAS Norfolk, Virginia for operational testing. Over the next seven months the prototype served with several other squadrons until it was assigned to VF-3 at NAS San Diego in December of 1941 for car-

The second production F4F-4 (BuNo 4059) on the ramp at Bethpage featured folding wings, six .50 caliber machine guns, modified cowling and a revised pitot tube. The darker half circle on the fuselage side below the wing trailing edge is a push-in foothold. (Grumman)

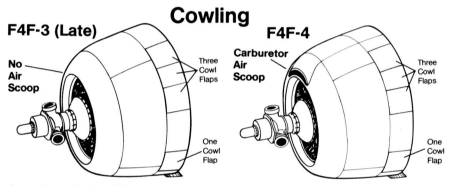

Cowling

F4F-3 (Late) — No Air Scoop — Three Cowl Flaps — One Cowl Flap

F4F-4 — Carburetor Air Scoop — Three Cowl Flaps — One Cowl Flap

An early production F4F-4 with the colorful insignia carried during 1942. Combat reports revealed that the Red center in the national insignia and Red rudder stripes could be mistaken for the Japanese 'meatball' insignia during the heat of battle. In May of 1942 BUAIR issued orders to delete the Red markings from all Navy aircraft. (Grumman)

The last production F4F-3 was modified with folding wings under the designation XF4F-4. In addition to the folding wing, the armament was changed from four .50 caliber machine guns to six. The prototype was evaluated by VF-42 at NAS Norfolk, Virginia during the Summer of 1941. (Grumman)

The small Red Boars Head and crest of VF-41, the 'Red Rippers', is barely visible below the cockpit of this F4F-4. VF-41 was assigned to USS RANGER (CV-4) during the Spring of 1942 and took part in the air battles over Algeria during the Allied invasion of North Africa. (NASM)

rier trials. The results of the operational tests were reported to the Bureau of Aeronautics on 11 December 1941 and concluded that while acceptable as a fighter, the XF4F-4 was noticeably more sluggish in flight than the F4F-3. The extra 400 pounds of wing fold mechanism and the extra two guns carried by the prototype had a significant effect on maneuverability and rate of climb.

Carrier trials were conducted by VF-3 on 6 and 7 January 1942 aboard USS SARA-TOGA. During the trials the XF4F-4 gained another 300 pounds of additional weight when armor plate was installed for pilot protection. VF-3 reported the heavy XF4F-4 was considerably inferior to the F4F-3 in speed, climb, and maneuverability. The squadron suggested that one way to reduce the weight of the XF4F-4 was to replace the hydraulic folding wings with lighter manual folding wings. With this modification the trail board recommended production of the XF4F-4.

The Navy awarded Grumman contracts for production of 1,169 XF4F-4s (with manually folding wings) under the designation F4F-4. The manual wing fold system on the production F4F-4 featured an access hole in the wing below the wing leading edge near the wing fold. A hand crank fitted into the opening engaging a gear that allowed the plane captain to easily raise or lower the wings.

Production F4F-4s began to reach first line Navy fighter squadrons after the Battle of the Coral Sea. The Coral Sea fighting had impressed the Navy with the need to enlarge shipboard fighter squadrons and as F4F-4s began reaching the fleet, squadron strength was boosted by fifty percent (from eighteen to twenty-seven aircraft per squadron). During May of 1942 squadrons in the Pacific began re-equipping with the F4F-4 often with mixed reactions. Pilots of VF-3 aboard USS YORKTOWN, VF-6 on USS ENTERPRISE and VF-8 aboard USS HORNET angrily complained about the F4F-4's reduced rate of climb, lower speed, sluggish maneuverability, and the lack of sustained fire power.

On the plus side the F4F-4 proved to be a stable gun platform and, as combat at Midway and Guadalcanal proved, the Wildcat's rugged construction could absorb a tremendous amount of battle damage and still fly. Navy and Marine pilots quickly developed tactics that took advantage of the Wildcat's strong points and turned the enemies weaknesses against him. During the Guadalcanal/Solomon Islands campaign Navy and Marine squadrons were made up entirely of F4F-4s. Grumman was turning out as many as 190 Wildcats per month and squadron strength steadily grew. By the end of 1942 Wildcat squadrons usually had a strength of thirty-six aircraft.

With the wings folded back the thirty-eight foot wingspan of the F4F-4 was reduced to fourteen feet four inches. The folding wing allowed the Navy to increase the number of fighters assigned to each squadron from eighteen to twenty-seven Wildcats per squadron. (D. Lucabaugh)

Ordnancemen aboard USS ENTERPRISE (CV-6) check the guns of an early F4F-4 of VF-6 on 10 April 1942. The bright Red and White rudder stripes have been covered with a dark canvas covering to camouflage them. (USN/D. Lucabaugh)

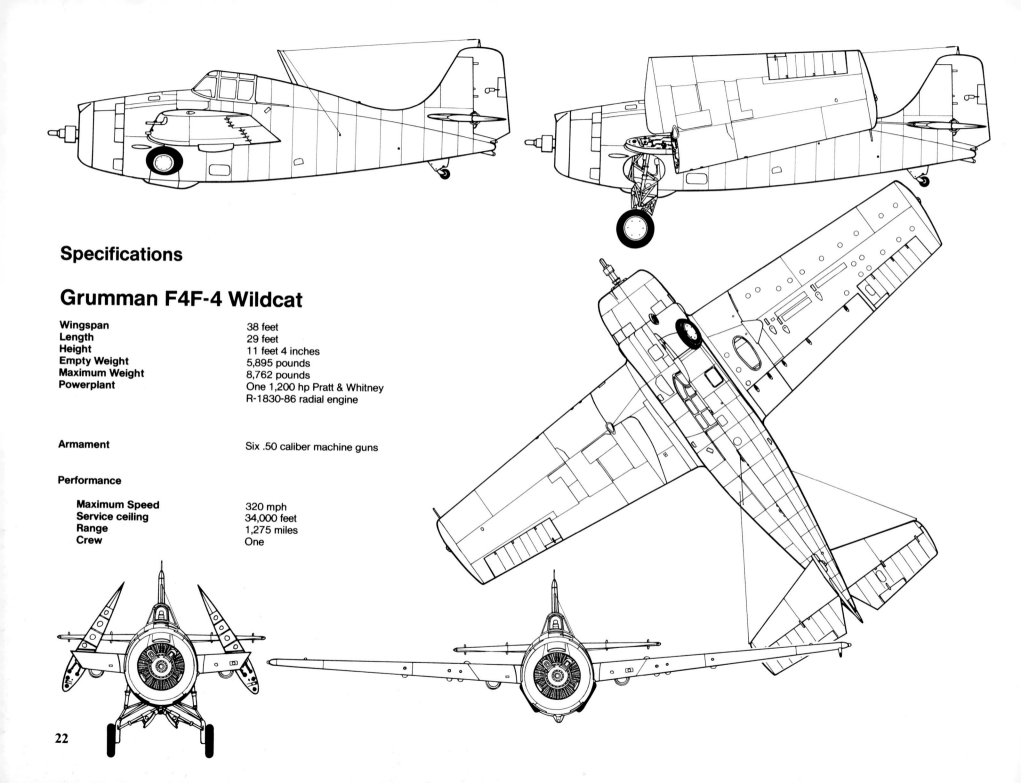

Specifications

Grumman F4F-4 Wildcat

Wingspan	38 feet
Length	29 feet
Height	11 feet 4 inches
Empty Weight	5,895 pounds
Maximum Weight	8,762 pounds
Powerplant	One 1,200 hp Pratt & Whitney R-1830-86 radial engine
Armament	Six .50 caliber machine guns

Performance

Maximum Speed	320 mph
Service ceiling	34,000 feet
Range	1,275 miles
Crew	One

The long distances separating the islands in the Solomons chain and the need for escort fighters prompted squadrons to develop field modifications to increase the range of the Wildcat. One such field modification was a forty-two gallon drop tank mounted on the fuselage centerline of the F4F-4 by VF-6 during May of 1942. The drop tank proved successful and was used in combat during the fighting at Guadalcanal. Pilots reported that the tank was adequate, however, many feared that a takeoff or landing accident with the centerline tank in place would be extremely hazardous.

The success of the field modified tank led to further development by the Bureau of Aeronautics which produced a jettisonable fifty-eight gallon drop tank that would be mounted under the wings instead of on the fuselage centerline. Grumman engineer Carl Anderson refined the installation and the two fifty-eight gallon tank system was standardized and put into production. The wing attachment brackets and necessary wing plumbing added another 750 pounds to the F4F-4, however, the trade off; range for speed and maneuverability, was generally felt to be acceptable. Field modification kits and drop tanks were rushed to the Pacific entering combat by late January of 1943. On one of their first missions with the new tanks VMF-121 and VMF-251 caught the Japanese by surprise off New Georgia and claimed twenty Japanese aircraft destroyed.

A number of F4F-4 variants were proposed by Grumman. The F4F-4A was a proposed engine change to the Pratt & Whitney R-1830-90, however, this order was cancelled before production was begun. The F4F-4B was an export designation for Wildcats supplied under Lend-Lease for the British Fleet Air Arm. The F4F-4P photo reconnaissance variant was similar to the F4F-3P with a small number being modified at Navy repair depots with a camera installed in the lower starboard fuselage side. A total of 1,169 F4F-4 Wildcats were produced by the end of 1942.

An F4F-4 with the revised national insignia carried after 15 May 1942 when the Navy issued ALNAV Dispatch 062230 which ordered the removal of the rudder stripes and the Red center circle from the national insignia. The national insignia is carried above and below each wing in addition to the fuselage sides. (Grumman)

Plane captains and ordnancemen preparing their F4F-4s for the first mission of the day, as deck handlers re-position Dauntless dive bombers aboard USS ENTERPRISE (CV-6) on 15 May 1942. The open panels on the wings of the second Wildcat are the gun bay access panels. (National Archives/D. Lucabaugh)

Armament

F4F-3

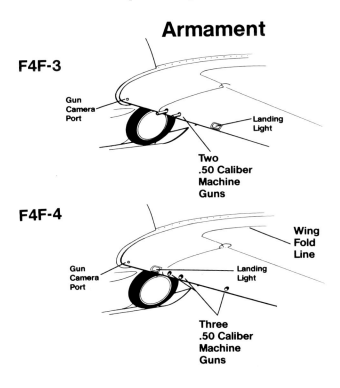

Gun Camera Port

Landing Light

Two .50 Caliber Machine Guns

F4F-4

Gun Camera Port

Wing Fold Line

Landing Light

Three .50 Caliber Machine Guns

Mechanics perform routine maintenance on a pair of F4F-4s in their camouflage net covered concrete revetment at Marine Corps Air Station Ewa, Hawaii during June of 1942. The mechanic working on the F4F-4 propeller in the background had to resort to an uncomfortable position to get the job done. (National Archives/D. Lucabaugh)

Crash crews spray water from a fire hose on the engine of an F4F-4 of VF-9 as it dangles over the side of USS RANGER (CV-4) on 25 August 1942. The tail hook and arresting cable are the only things keeping the Wildcat from going into the water. (USN/D. Lucabaugh)

This damaged Marine Wildcat being cannibalized for parts on Midway Island during June of 1942, was one of the survivors of VMF-221's attack against the first Japanese raid on Midway. The Marines lost fifteen F2A-3s and F4F-4s during the action and of the survivors only two Wildcats and a few Buffalos were fit for action.

This F4F-4 of VF-41 crash landed aboard USS RANGER (CV-4) during June of 1942. The landing gear was ripped off and a fire had started under the aircraft from spilled fuel. The pilot has already left the cockpit as a crewman moves in to fight the fire with a portable fire extinguisher. (National Archives/D. Lucabaugh)

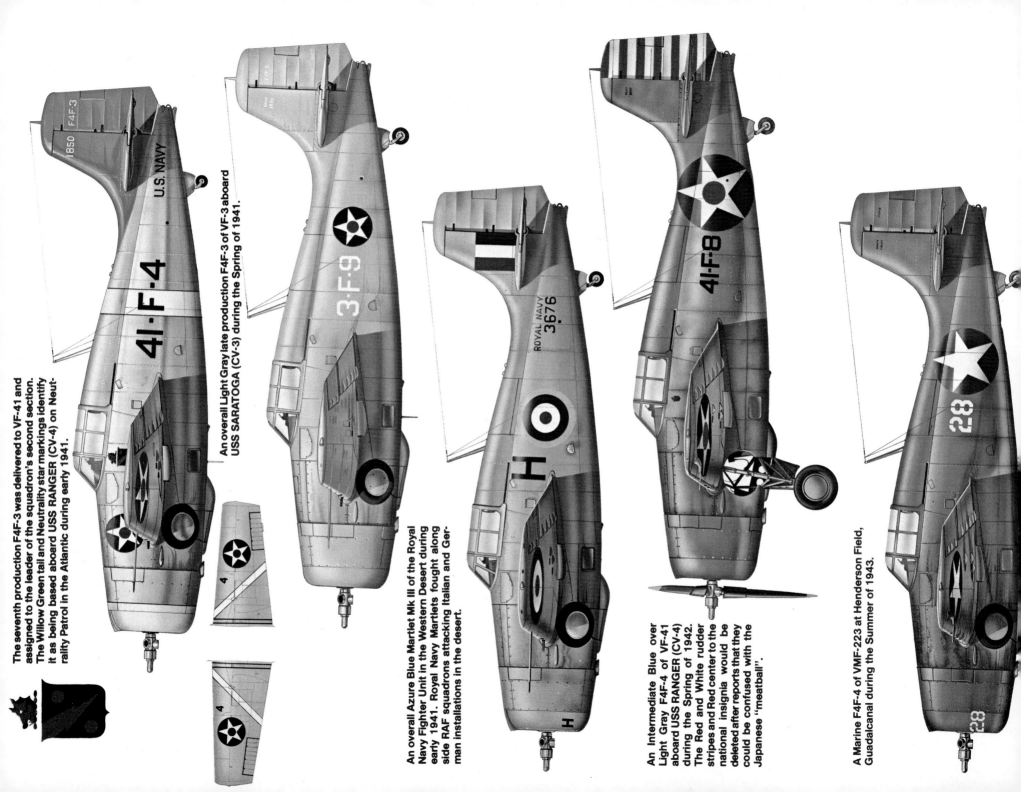

The seventh production F4F-3 was delivered to VF-41 and assigned to the leader of the squadron's second section. The Willow Green tail and Neutrality star markings identify it as being based aboard USS RANGER (CV-4) on Neutrality Patrol in the Atlantic during early 1941.

An overall Light Gray late production F4F-3 of VF-3 aboard USS SARATOGA (CV-3) during the Spring of 1941.

An overall Azure Blue Martlet Mk III of the Royal Navy Fighter Unit in the Western Desert during early 1941. Royal Navy Martlets fought alongside RAF squadrons attacking Italian and German installations in the desert.

An Intermediate Blue over Light Gray F4F-4 of VF-41 aboard USS RANGER (CV-4) during the Spring of 1942. The Red and White rudder stripes and Red center to the national insignia would be deleted after reports that they could be confused with the Japanese "meatball".

A Marine F4F-4 of VMF-223 at Henderson Field, Guadalcanal during the Summer of 1943.

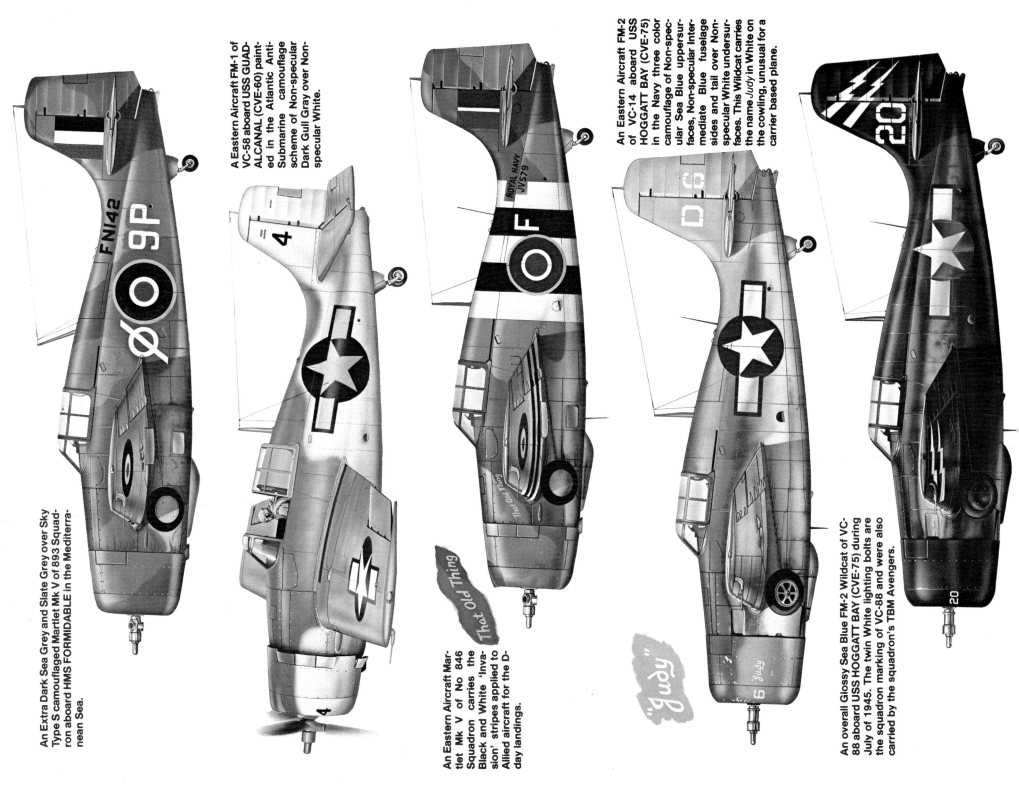

An Extra Dark Sea Grey and Slate Grey over Sky Type S camouflaged Martlet Mk V of 893 Squadron aboard HMS FORMIDABLE in the Mediterranean Sea.

A Eastern Aircraft FM-1 of VC-58 aboard USS GUADALCANAL (CVE-60) painted in the Atlantic Anti-Submarine camouflage scheme of Non-specular Dark Gull Gray over Non-specular White.

An Eastern Aircraft FM-2 of VC-14 aboard USS HOGGATT BAY (CVE-75) in the Navy three color camouflage of Non-specular Sea Blue uppersurfaces, Non-specular Intermediate Blue fuselage sides and tail over Non-specular White undersurfaces. This Wildcat carries the name *Judy* in White on the cowling, unusual for a carrier based plane.

An Eastern Aircraft Martlet Mk V of No 846 Squadron carries the Black and White 'Invasion' stripes applied to Allied aircraft for the D-day landings.

An overall Glossy Sea Blue FM-2 Wildcat of VC-88 aboard USS HOGGATT BAY (CVE-75) during July of 1945. The twin White lighting bolts are the squadron marking of VC-88 and were also carried by the squadron's TBM Avengers.

An F4F with underwing fifty-eight gallon fuel tanks prepares to take off from USS RANGER during OPERATION TORCH. During the Invasion of North Africa Wildcat pilots found themselves fighting traditional American allies, the French, flying American-built Curtiss Hawk 75 (P-36) fighters. (Don Spering/AIR)

Marines on Guadalcanal use a CO_2 fire extinguisher and sand to save a Wildcat set afire by a near miss from a Japanese bombing raid shortly after the Marine Wildcats arrived on the island on 20 August 1942. (NASM)

An F4F-4 on patrol off Guadalcanal on 6 April 1943. The dark circles around the national insignia are the painted out Yellow surround that was added to aircraft participating in the invasion of North Africa. An Indian headdress personal marking is painted on the fuselage just below the windscreen. (National Archives/D. Lucabaugh)

Wildcats of either VF-41 or VF-9 line the deck edge aboard USS RANGER as ordnancemen test fire the guns prior to beginning operations during OPERATION TORCH. The Wildcat in the foreground is hooked to the tow tractor by a tow bar attached to the towing lug mounted on the fuselage below the tailhook. (National Archives)

27

A Marine F4F-4 returns from a combat patrol over Guadalcanal during December of 1942. The crushed coral runways and taxiways were hard on the Wildcats, dust clogged engine filters and stones thrown up by the prop wash chipped the propeller blades and wing leading edges. (National Archives/D. Lucabaugh)

Pitot Tube

F4F-3

Straight Pitot Tube

F4F-4

L-Shaped Pitot Tube

Marine Wildcats line the dirt taxiway of Henderson Field, Guadalcanal on 15 November 1943. Conditions on Guadalcanal were harsh and primitive. The tents among the palm trees in the background are the living quarters for the Marine pilots. (Don Spering/AIR)

Marines of VMO-251 work on their Wildcats under the palm trees at Espiritu Santo, New Hebrides on 10 April 1943. VMO-251 flew a mix of F4F-3Ps, F4F-4s and F4F-7s and many of its pilots were used to reinforce the hard pressed squadrons on Guadalcanal. (National Archives/D. Lucabaugh)

The tailhook of this F4F-4 of VF-9 is about to catch an arresting cable aboard USS RANGER (CV-4) on 22 October 1942. The retractable tail hook is painted White with Black bands. (National Archives/D. Lucabaugh)

An F4F-4 Wildcat of Armed Observation Squadron 28 (VGF-28) climbs out after launching from USS CHARGER (CVE-30) on 10 October 1942. The squadron codes are carried on the fuselage side in Non-specular Black. (National Archives/D. Lucabaugh)

A wave washes over the bow of the plane guard destroyer as USS RANGER (CV-4) turns into the wind to begin flight operations during August of 1942. First to launch will be two divisions of VF-9 F4F-4s which will orbit the ships on combat air patrol to defend the task force. (National Archives/D. Lucabaugh)

Aircraft handlers wait under the wings of their assigned aircraft for the signal to pull the wheel chocks of these F4F-4s warming up for their next mission. The removable wing bomb rack was capable of carrying bombs up to 100 pounds. (USN/D. Lucabaugh)

The ship's crane hoists an F4F-4 of VF-41 aboard USS Ranger (CV-4) at NAS Norfolk Virginia during August of 1942. The Wildcat's sling hoist eye is located just in front of the windscreen. The sailor in the cockpit is the plane captain, who will control the Wildcat's brakes when the aircraft is maneuvered into the ship's hangar bay. (National Archives/D. Lucabaugh)

A non-operational F4F-4 is re-painted in preparation for use in a War Bond rally during September of 1942. The wing gun ports have been sealed over and the gunsight has been removed. The landing gear has been re-painted in Green Zink Cromate, however, operational Wildcats usually had the landing gear painted Black. (USN/D. Lucabaugh)

The use of a White individual aircraft number on the fuselage of this F4F-4 of VGF-29 aboard USS SANTEE (CVE-29) is unusual. VGF squadrons spotted gunfire for battleships and cruisers during shore bombardments. (USN/D. Lucabaugh)

A Wildcat makes an arrested landing aboard USS RANGER on 15 October 1942. If the tail hook had missed the arresting wire, the Wildcat would have gone into the crash barrier rigged just in front of the aircraft. (National Archives. D. Lucabaugh)

A group of mechanics studies the engine of an F4F-4 of Armed Scouting Squadron (VGS) 30 at NAS Norfolk during September of 1942. The squadron codes and oversized national insignia are carried much further back on the fuselage than normal. Warming up alongside the Wildcat is a Royal Navy Tarpon Mk 1 (TBF Avenger). (USN/D. Lucabaugh)

Ordnancemen boresight the .50 caliber Browning machine guns on an F4F-4 shortly before the Allied landings in North Africa. A Yellow surround has been added to the fuselage national insignia as a recognition aid. All aircraft taking part in OPERATION TORCH carried this marking. (NASM)

An F4F-4 of VF-20 takes off from USS BARNES (CVE-20) 26 March 1943. The cable hanging from the Wildcat's tail hook is the catapult hold back cable which held the aircraft in position while the engine was brought to full power prior to launch. The cable was designed to brake when the catapult fired. (National Archives/D. Lucabaugh)

This F4F-4 struck the bow 40mm Bofors guns on take off nearly severing the starboard wing tip. The pilot was able to successfully ditch the Wildcat and was picked up by the plane guard destroyer. (National Archives/D. Lucabaugh)

The gun bay access panels of this F4F-4 on board USS LONG ISLAND (CVE-1) during March of 1943 have been sealed with tape to keep out moisture. USS LONG ISLAND was the prototype escort carrier and lacked the traditional "island" found on all fleet carriers and later escort carriers. She was used primarily as both a training carrier and aircraft transport. (NASM)

31

An F4F-4 of VF-22 in the three tone camouflage finish of Semi-Gloss Sea Blue, Non-specular Intermediate Blue over Non-specular White undersurfaces is maneuvered off the elevator aboard USS INDEPENDENCE (CVL-22) on 30 April 1943. The jury struts securing the folded wings to the horizontal stabilizer were stored in the aircraft baggage compartment when not in use. (USN/D. Lucabaugh)

Ground crewmen unfold the wings of an F4F-4 at a Naval Air Station. When not in use the hand crank folded back into the open bay on the underside of the wing leading edge. This Wildcat has the national insignia bordered in Blue while the F4F in the background has the national insignia bordered in Red. (NASM)

Wing Fold

F4F-4

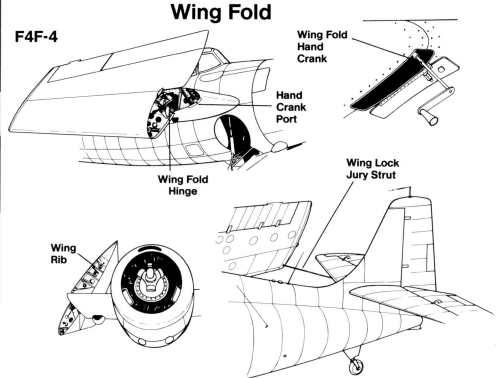

Wing Fold Hand Crank

Hand Crank Port

Wing Fold Hinge

Wing Lock Jury Strut

Wing Rib

F4F-4 (BuNo 5262) was the 233rd F4F-4 built and was retained at Grumman for modification with full span flaps. The modification proved unnecessary and was not adopted for production Wildcats. The combination of Red and White rudder stripes with the Blue and White national insignia is unusual. (National Archives. D. Lucabaugh)

58 Gallon External Tank

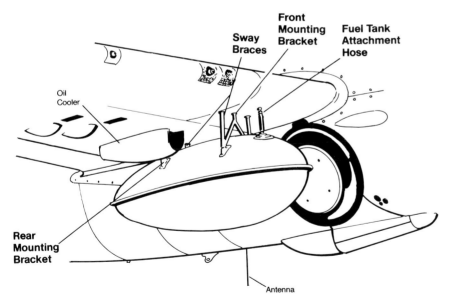

A division of F4F-4s on patrol above the clouds during mid-1943. The national insignia has the Red surround first introduced on 29 June 1943 and used between July and October of 1943. (USN)

The catapult tow bridle is attached to the landing gear of an F4F-4 as it prepares to launch on an anti-submarine patrol from USS SANTEE (CVE-29) during November of 1943. The Wildcat is camouflaged in the Atlantic anti-submarine scheme of Dark Gull Gray upper surfaces and Insignia White undersurfaces. (National Archives/D. Lucabaugh)

F4F-7

To cover the long distances between islands in the Pacific, the Navy realized that a dedicated carrier based long range photo reconnaissance aircraft was needed. In early 1941 Grumman began development of a long range Wildcat photo reconnaissance variant. A standard F4F-4 airframe was modified to serve as the prototype under the designation F4F-7.

The wing fold mechanism and armament was removed and the wing sealed to serve as a fuel tank capable of holding 555 gallons of fuel. The camera was installed in the fuselage behind the cockpit replacing the reserve fuselage fuel tank with the camera window installed in the belly. A pair of fuel jettison pipes were installed at the base of the rudder to allow the pilot to dump excess fuel and lower the Wildcat's landing weight when returning from a mission. The forward canopy section was modified with the flat armor glass windshield being replaced by a smoothly curved plexiglass windshield.

The prototype made its first flight on 30 December 1941, being delivered to NAS Anacostia two weeks later. After a successful evaluation by the trials board at Anacostia the Navy placed production contracts for over one hundred F4F-7s. In the event only twenty-one F4F-7s were actually produced, the remainder being completed as F4F-3s and issued to Training Command as advanced trainers. Production F4F-7s were fitted with an autopilot to ease pilot workload on long range flights. With a total fuel capacity of 685 gallons the F4F-7 could stay aloft for up to twenty-four hours and had a range of 3,700 miles. One record breaking cross-country endurance flight was flown by LCDR Andy Jackson, who flew an F4F-7 non-stop from New York to Los Angeles, over 3,000 miles, in eleven hours. This unheard of feat for a fighter aircraft was kept a secret because of wartime security and the record was never officially claimed. When the flight plan for the non-stop flight was filed with the Army in New York, the Army flight clearance personnel called back stating that it had to be a mistake. The wisecracking Navy controller was reported to have responded *"...The flight plan is correct; all Navy fighters have a 3,000 mile range...."*

The F4F-7 was introduced into combat at Guadalcanal by LT Herman Hanson, the staff photo pilot of the First Marine Air Wing. Operating with two F4F-7s LT Hanson flew reconnaissance missions from Guadalcanal far up the 'Slot' to Munda and beyond. The original two F4F-7s were eventually destroyed during Japanese air raids on Henderson Field, however, they were quickly replaced by aircraft from Marine Observation Squadron 251 (VMO-251)at Espiritu. VMO-251 operated a mix of F4F-7s, F4F-3Ps, and F4F-4s obtaining replacement aircraft from Navy carrier air groups in the vicinity. Each carrier had one F4F-7 assigned, although these aircraft were normally put ashore at Espiritu since the carriers had little need for them. These F4F-7s became the source of spare aircraft and parts for Hanson's one man photo unit. After flying over 100 missions, Hansen contracted malaria and was rotated to New Zealand ending the use of the F4F-7 at Guadalcanal. Reportedly the aircraft that survived were later re-converted to the F4F-3 configuration at Navy repair depots during 1943.

The F4F-7 was fitted with two emergency fuel dump pipes mounted at the base of the rudder above the tail hook. Two F4F-7s were flown in combat at Guadalcanal by LT Herman Hanson, staff photo pilot for the First Marine Air Wing at Henderson Field. (Don Spering/AIR)

Fuel Dump Pipes

Canopy

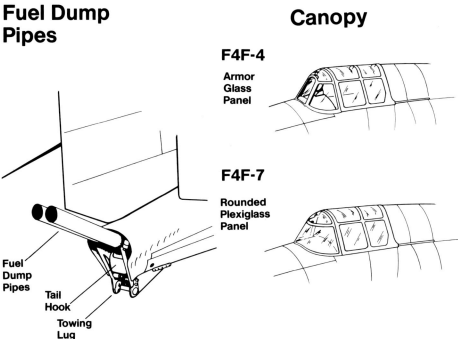

F4F-4

Armor Glass Panel

F4F-7

Rounded Plexiglass Panel

Fuel Dump Pipes

Tail Hook

Towing Lug

(Left) The F4F-7 was a photo reconnaissance variant of the F4F-4 with a camera mounted behind the pilot in place of the emergency fuel tank. All armament was removed, the wings sealed and filled with fuel. During 1942 an F4F-7 broke the endurance record for single engine fighters when it made a non-stop flight from New York to Los Angeles in eleven hours. (Don Spering/AIR)

G-36B/Martlet Mk II

During early 1940, the British Purchasing Commission had placed an order with Grumman for 100 export Wildcats powered by the 1,200 hp Pratt & Whitney S3C4-G engine driving an uncuffed Hamilton Standard propeller under the Grumman export designation G-36B (British designation Martlet Mk I). Shortly after this order was placed, however, the British learned that the folding wing XF4F-4 had made its first flight. The Fleet Arm Arm immediately recognized the advantages that the folding wing would have on the crowded decks of their carriers and wanted the folding wing incorporated on the G-36B, even if it meant a delay in deliveries. Negotiations between the US Navy, Grumman, and the British resulted in an amended contract that included the folding wing.

Before the negotiations were completed, he first ten G-36Bs had been completed by Grumman with fixed wings. The British agreed to take delivery of these aircraft with the understanding that they would be retro-fitted with folding wings at a later date. The remaining ninety aircraft would be similar to the F4F-4 with folding wings and an armament of six .50 caliber machine guns mounted in the wings. The cowling was modified to accept the Pratt & Whitney S3C4-G engine with the carburetor air scoop being deleted. A single double wide cowl flap was installed on each side of the cowling replacing the eight cowl flaps of the F4F-4 cowl. Since the FAA had already taken delivery of the ex-French G-36As under the designation Martlet I, the contract was further modified changing the designation of the G-36B to Martlet Mk II. The first ten aircraft delivered were known as non-standard Martlet Mk IIs until they were modified with folding wings.

The first ten fixed wing non-standard Martlet Mk IIs were delivered to the British between October of 1940 and April of 1941, followed by the first folding wing Martlet Mk II in August. Forty-six were delivered to England, while the remaining fifty-four were sent directly to India for service in the Far East. The first British Martlet IIs to serve at sea were assigned to No 802 Squadron aboard HMS AUDACITY during September of 1942. The first victory by a shipboard Martlet II occurred during this deployment when a Martlet on combat air patrol shot down a German Fw 200 bomber on 20 September.

A Martlet Mk II prepares for take off aboard a British aircraft carrier during late 1942. Most Martlet Mk IIs were shipped directly to India where they were assembled and used in combat in the Indian Ocean Theater of Operations. (IWM/R.Dorr)

Ground crews warm up the engines of three Martlet Mk IIs on an English airfield. Martlet Mk IIs were similar to US Navy F4F-4s with folding wings and six .50 caliber machine guns. Royal Navy Martlets were painted in Extra Dark Sea Grey and Slate Grey uppersurfaces over Sky type S undersurfaces. (F.A.A. Museum)

Cowling

F4F-4

Air Scoop

Cowl Flaps

Martlet II

No Air Scoop

Double Wide Cowl Flap

Propeller

F4F-4

Propeller Hub

Cuffed Curtiss Electric Propeller

Martlet II

Propeller Hub

Uncuffed Hamilton Standard Propeller

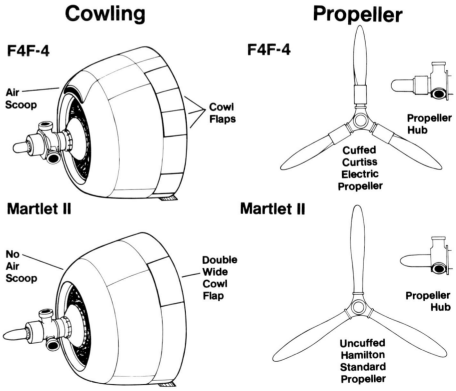

Martlet Mk IV

With the passage of the Lend-Lease Act and US entry into the Second World War large numbers of American built aircraft were supplied to the British. Among the earliest Lend-Lease deliveries were 220 Wildcats built under the US Navy export designation F4F-4B. Designated Martlet Mk IV by the Fleet Air Arm, these first Lend-Lease Martlets were identical to the F4F-4 except for the engine and cowling. The Martlet IV was powered by a nine cylinder 1,200 Wright R-1820-40B radial engine similar to the R-1820-G205 engine used in the Martlet Mk I. The cowling differed considerably from the F4F-4 cowl; being rounder and narrower in chord, with the carburetor air scoop deleted. A single double wide cowl flap mounted high on the rear of the cowling replaced the eight smaller cowl flaps of the F4F-4 and the cuffed Curtiss Electric propeller was replaced by an uncuffed Hamilton Standard propeller.

The first Martlet Mk IVs were delivered to No 892 Squadron at Naval Air Station Norfolk, Virginia on 15 July 1942, deploying aboard HMS ARCHER a short time later. Besides fleet air defense, the Martlet IVs were used as escorts for Avengers, Barracudas and Swordfish torpedo bombers both on anti-submarine missions and attacks against enemy surface shipping. The Mk IV served, for the most part, aboard escort carriers operating in the Atlantic and Mediterranean.

A number of Royal Navy squadrons, however, participated in Pacific Theater operations during the British landings on Madagascar, and when HMS ILLUSTRIOUS in company with HMS FORMIDABLE, conducted a diversionary thrust into the Bay of Bengal off India. The diversion was intended to draw Japanese attention away from US Marine Corps landings in the Solomons. During this operation a pair of Martlet IVs of No 888 Squadron aboard HMS ILLUSTRIOUS scored the only Martlet victory over a Japanese aircraft, when they shot down a Kawanishi H6K Mavis reconnaissance flying boat. During May through July of 1943 thirty-six Martlet IVs were embarked aboard HMS VICTORIOUS for joint British/American operations in the South Pacific alongside the American carrier USS SARATOGA. The two carriers operated in the Middle Solomon Islands area in June of 1943 with Martlets from HMS VICTORIOUS providing task force air cover, while Wildcats from USS SARATOGA escorted TBM Avenger torpedo bombers and SBD Dauntless dive bombers in attacks against Japanese shore positions.

The first Martlet Mk IV (FN100) came off the Grumman production line on 27 February 1942. Martlet Mk IVs were powered by a Wright R-1820-40B engine housed in a rounded narrow chord cowling. (Grumman)

Cowling

F4F-4

Air Scoop

Three Cowl Flaps

Cowl Flap

Martlet IV

No Air Scoop

Single Double Wide Cowl Flap

(Left) A Martlet Mk IV (FN142) of No 893 Squadron takes off from HMS FORMIDABLE in the Mediterranean Sea. The wire running from the tip of the stabilizer to the roundel is the IFF antenna aerial. (IWM/R.Dorr)

Eastern Aircraft FM-1

By late June 1942, Grumman was heavily engaged in production of the F4F-4 Wildcat, TBF Avenger, J2F Duck, J4F Widgeon and was tooling-up to build the Wildcat's successor — the F6F-3 Hellcat. The Navy decided that production of the F6F Hellcat should have top priority and, since Grumman had reached its maximum production capacity, another manufacturer for both the F4F-4 and TBF-1 Avenger would have to be found.

When war was declared on 8 December 1941, the General Motors Corporation ceased all automobile production, idling its five east coast auto plants. General Motors felt that these idle plants could be put to use supporting the war effort by manufacturing aircraft spare parts. During early 1942 the Navy Department arranged a meeting between representatives of General Motors and Grumman with the idea that General Motors could take some of the production burden from the overtaxed Grumman facilities at Bethpage.

The General Motors (GM) representatives were surprised to find that Grumman was seeking additional factory space for full scale aircraft production rather than a simple spare parts manufacturing agreement. GM engineers visited Grumman to study aircraft production techniques and Grumman engineers traveled to GM plants to assist in the enormous job of reorganizing the automobile plants for aircraft production. By mid-1942 all five GM plants had been completely reorganized, becoming the Eastern Aircraft Division of the General Motors Corporation.

An FM-1 of VGF-29 is manhandled into position on the catapult aboard USS SANTEE (CVE-29) during November of 1943. The Wildcats of VGF-29 were teamed with TBM Avengers of VGS-29 to form an escort carrier air group for anti-submarine operations in the Atlantic. (National Archives)

The first Eastern Aircraft produced FM-1 underwent testing at NAS Anacostia during the Spring of 1942. The armament of the FM-1 was reduced to four .50 caliber machine guns and ammunition loads were increased. The White "FT" (Flight Test) marking on the cowling was common to aircraft involved in flight testing. (NASM)

Under the terms of the agreement between the Navy, Grumman, and Eastern Aircraft, Eastern would build the F4F Wildcat and TBF Avenger under license from Grumman. Initially Eastern received ten sets of F4F-4 sub-assemblies and specially configured "PK" aircraft to be used as training aids. The "PK" aircraft were standard F4F-4s assembled with Parker-Kalon (PK) fasteners instead of rivets. These aircraft could be easily disassembled and re-assembled for study.

An FM-1 (BuNo 46776) of VC-58 narrowly missed going off the deck of USS GUADALCANAL (CVE-60) on 13 January 1944. The Wildcat is painted in the Atlantic anti-submarine camouflage scheme of Non-specular Dark Gull Gray over Non-specular Insignia White with aircraft numbers in Non-specular Black. (USN/D. Lucabaugh)

Armament

Eastern's Linden, New Jersey plant was responsible for Wildcat production, building the F4F-4 under the designation FM-1 Wildcat. The first FM-1, assembled from Grumman supplied parts, made its first flight on 1 September 1942. By the end of 1942 a total of twenty-one FM-1s had been delivered to the Navy and production was rapidly increasing. During 1943 Eastern was given responsibility for all future Wildcat production freeing Grumman to concentrate on production of the Hellcat.

The Grumman F4F-4 and Eastern FM-1 were identical except for armament. Acting on complaints from front line combat pilots the Bureau of Aeronautics (BUAIR) had been trying to resolve the ammunition problem with the F4F-4. One suggestion from combat veterans was passed along to the Fleet as an interim measure while BUAIR worked on the problem. The guns on the F4F-4 could be selectivity fired and a number of combat pilots had begun holding back the two outboard .50 caliber machine guns as a "get me home" reserve. While this did not solve the problem it did prolong firing time.

The Navy continued to work with Grumman to redesign the folding wings to accommodate a four gun installation with greater ammunition loads. The British, however, held fast to their requirement for a three gun battery in each wing. The need to maintain a standardized Grumman production line prevented any change during late 1941 and early 1942.

When Wildcat production shifted from Grumman to Eastern Aircraft the Navy decided that the Eastern Aircraft produced Wildcat variant would incorporate the armament change. On 14 June 1942 the Navy issued a production change order instructing Eastern to begin building the FM-1 with the four gun wing armament, commencing with the eleventh FM-1 off the production line. From this point on all FM-1s were produced with the four gun installation. A total of 909 FM-1s were produced by Eastern Aircraft before production shifted to a light weight variant of the Wildcat.

F4F-4

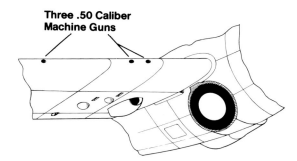

Three .50 Caliber Machine Guns

FM-1

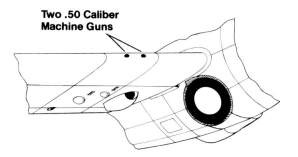

Two .50 Caliber Machine Guns

(Above) Deck handlers reposition an FM-1 of VC-33 on the pitching deck of USS NASSAU (CVE-16) on 6 September 1943. With the exception of the armament carried, the FM-1 was identical to the F4F-4. A faintly visible previous squadron code (A-25) has been painted out on the starboard wing. (USN/D. Lucabaugh)

(Below) An FM-1 of VC-12 goes out of control, nearly dragging its starboard wing tip, after a bad landing aboard USS Core (CVE-13). The narrow track of the Wildcat's landing gear made landings difficult and a burst of power on landing could quickly throw the Wildcat out of control. The squadron insignia on the fuselage side is a Black and White cat with its long tail forming a circle around it. (USN/D. Lucabaugh)

Martlet V

When production of the F4F-4 and Martlet IV was transferred to Eastern Aircraft in early 1942, the British were allotted 312 aircraft from the FM-1 production line under Lend-Lease. Designated the Martlet Mk V (British serials JV325-JV636), these aircraft were built to US Navy specifications and were identical to the FM-1. Of the 312 Martlet Vs on order, 311 were eventually received by the British. Two aircraft were delivered in late 1942, 309 were delivered in 1943, and one was destroyed in a post-production test flight and was not replaced.

The Martlet Mk.V was mainly employed on British escort carriers in the Atlantic and Mediterranean. Normal Fleet Air Arm practice was to embark a squadron consisting of four to six Martlets and up to twelve anti-submarine aircraft such as the Avenger, Barracuda, or Swordfish aboard each escort carrier. In addition to providing fighter protection for the task force, the Wildcats worked with the ASW aircraft providing flak suppression during attacks on German U-boats.

Two Martlet V squadrons embarked aboard HMS PURSUER and HMS SEARCHER took part in OPERATON TUNGSTEN, the attack on the German pocket battleship TIRPITZ. The Martlets flew flak suppression for Barracuda dive bombers during the attack. Although the attack failed to destroy the battleship, the damage inflicted on TIRPITZ kept her out of action for several months. Martlet V equipped squadrons flying from HMS ILLUSTRIOUS also took part in the Allied amphibious assault at Salerno, Italy providing fighter cover for both the invasion fleet and over the beachhead.

Deck crews spread the wings of a Martlet Mk V of No 861 Squadron aboard HMS PURSER in the North Atlantic during early 1945. Royal Navy Martlets were used for air defense against German Fw 200 bombers and in anti-submarine teams with Swordfish, Barracuda or Avenger ASW aircraft. (F.A.A. Museum)

A Martlet Mk V of No 846 Squadron carries the White and Black stripes added to Allied aircraft for the D-day landings on 6 June 1944. Barely visible on the fuselage above the wing leading edge is the name *That Old Thing* in White. (Ray Sturtivant)

A Martlet Mk V (JV394) of No 842 Squadron on deck alert aboard HMS FENCER during the Summer of 1944. The pilot Sub LT Dennis White has rigged an umbrella to protect himself from the hot sun in the Bay of Biscay. LT White is now CDR White RN (Retired), Director of the Fleet Air Arm Museum. (F.A.A. Museum)

XF4F-8

F4F-4 Wildcat production ended at Grumman when the last production run of 100 F4F-4s was completed in May of 1943. Before production ceased, however, two prototypes of a light weight variant of the Wildcat were built under the designation XF4F-8. The Navy requested a light weight Wildcat for operations from small escort carriers and Grumman made every effort to lower the gross weight of the F4F-4 to improve performance and deck handling qualities.

The XF4F-8 was powered by an experimental 1,300 hp single stage two speed supercharged Curtiss XR-1820-56 Cyclone radial engine driving an uncuffed Hamilton Standard constant speed propeller. The Curtiss engine featured forged cylinder heads that reduced engine weight by 230 pounds while providing an additional 150 horsepower over the earlier Pratt and Whitney R-1830-86 engine. The engine change made it necessary to redesign the cowling. A round narrow chord cowling (similar to that of the Martlet Mk V) with a single double wide cowl flap high on the rear of the cowling was fitted to the XF4F-8. The two exhaust stubs of the F4F-4 were replaced with direct jet type exhaust ports. One set of exhaust ports were mounted below the cowl flap on each side of the fuselage at the rear of the cowling and two sets were mounted on the underside of the fuselage just behind the cowling.

Cowling

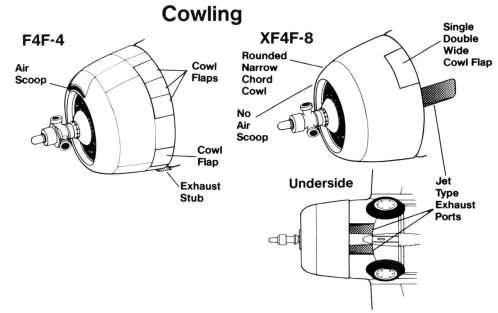

F4F-4 — Air Scoop, Cowl Flaps, Cowl Flap, Exhaust Stub

XF4F-8 — Rounded Narrow Chord Cowl, No Air Scoop, Single Double Wide Cowl Flap, Jet Type Exhaust Ports

Underside

The first light weight XF4F-8 prototype (BuNo 12228) on the ramp at Bethpage on 12 November 1943. Slotted flaps were tested on the XF4F-8, however, the standard F4F wing flaps proved to be superior and were later retrofitted to the prototype. (Grumman)

The second XF4F-8 prototype featured an eight and one half inch extension to the vertical fin and rudder made necessary by the increased torque of the 1,300 hp Curtiss XR-1820-56 engine. (Grumman)

The XF4F-8 prototype was powered by a 1,300 hp Curtiss XR-1820-56 engine driving an uncuffed Hamilton Standard propeller with direct jet type exhaust ports replacing the two exhaust stubs of the FM-1. The XF4F-8 was ordered into production at Eastern Aircraft under the designation FM-2. (Grumman)

The first prototype was fitted with a standard F4F-4 fin and rudder, however, the torque from the more powerful Curtiss engine made it necessary to increase the height of the fin and rudder to restore lateral stability. The first XF4F-8 (BuNo 12228) made its maiden flight on 8 November 1942 at Bethpage. Following factory tests the prototype was delivered to NAS Anacostia the following month. The second XF4F-8 (BuNo 12229) was retained at Bethpage by Grumman for additional testing.

The XF4F-8s were initially fitted with slotted wing flaps, however, early flight tests revealed that the standard F4F split trailing edge flaps were superior and these were retrofitted to both prototypes. The engine oil coolers were repositioned from the wing to inside the cowling and the underwing oil coolers were removed. The armament of the XF4F-8 consisted of four .50 caliber machine guns mounted in the wings with provision for 430 rounds of ammunition per gun. The weight saving efforts by Grumman engineers were successful, gross weight for the XF4F-8 prototypes was 5,542 pounds, 530 pounds less than a standard F4F-4.

Flight tests with the XF4F-8 revealed that while it was only slightly faster than an F4F-4, the rate of climb had increased approximately 1,000 feet per minute, range was increased over 100 miles, and maneuverability was considerably better. Service ceiling was raised from 33,700 feet to 35,600 feet, although performance at altitude suffered because of the single stage supercharger of the Curtiss engine. The XF4F-8 successfully completed its evaluation during early 1943 and the Navy ordered the XF4F-8 into production by Eastern Aircraft under the designation FM-2.

Fin and Rudder

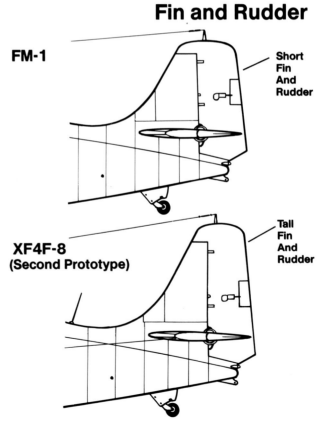

FM-1

Short Fin And Rudder

XF4F-8
(Second Prototype)

Tall Fin And Rudder

Eastern Aircraft FM-2

The first production FM-2 came off the Eastern line during mid 1943 and by the end of the year 310 aircraft had been accepted by the Navy. Production rapidly picked up and during 1944 deliveries were averaging over 200 FM-2s per month. By the end of 1944 a total of 2,890 FM-2 Wildcats were produced at the Linden plant.

While retaining the tall fin and rudder of the second XF4F-8 prototype, production FM-2 Wildcats incorporated a number of changes and improvements over the prototype. A production 1,350 hp Curtiss R-1820-56W engine featuring water injection was installed in place of the experimental XR-1820-56. The water injection system boosted engine power from the Curtiss engine for short periods under emergency conditions. An uncuffed Curtiss Electric propeller replaced the Hamilton Standard propeller of the prototypes and a straight radio antenna mast was installed replacing the forward raked radio antenna mast found on all previous F4Fs.

By the time the FM-2 was introduced into squadron service during late 1943, the Grumman F6F Hellcat and Vought F4U Corsair had replaced the F4F-4 as the Navy's first-line carrier based fighter. FM-2s were normally assigned to Composite (VC) squadrons where they operated alongside TBM Avengers. Flying from small escort carriers, the missions of the VC squadrons varied considerably. When part of an amphibious task force, Wildcats were responsible for providing air support to the Marines ashore and anti-submarine patrols (teamed with Avengers) to protect the force from prowling Japanese submarines. The FM-2 units were also given the responsibility for air defense of the amphibious landing force freeing the fleet carriers with their F6F Hellcats and F4U Corsairs to engage in offensive operations further at sea. While opportunities for air combat were limited, by the end of the war FM-2 pilots had been credited with 422 Japanese aircraft destroyed in air to air combat.

To improve the FM-2s firepower in the ground support and anti-submarine roles, Eastern modified an FM-2 with three Mk 5 zero-length rocket launcher stubs for 5 inch high velocity aircraft rockets (HVAR) under each outer wing panel. The modification proved successful and the last 1,400 FM-2s off the Linden production line were fitted with the rocket launcher stubs. These late model FM-2s saw action during the invasions of the Philippines and Okinawa, performing vital air support missions for the Marines ashore. On 5 August 1945 an FM-2 of VC-98 flying from the USS LUNGA operating off the Japanese home islands scored the last Wildcat victory of the war — a Francis reconnaissance bomber.

During May of 1945 the Navy accepted the last sixty FM-2 Wildcats and production of the Wildcat came to a halt. Production of the FM-2 variant had totaled 4,777 aircraft, over forty percent of the 7,251 Wildcats produced by both Grumman and Eastern. When the war ended the Wildcat quickly disappeared from Navy squadrons; some were put in storage, while others were sold as military surplus, none saw active post war service. The Wildcat had been the right aircraft at the right time, but had outlived its usefulness. In 1945 a new chapter in naval aviation history was about to begin with the introduction of jet fighters — the Wildcat's five year Navy career had come to an end.

Production FM-2s retained the tall tail tested on the second XF4F-8 prototype. FM-2s were the most widely produced variant of the Wildcat with over 4,400 being built before production was terminated in late 1945. (Don Spering/AIR)

An FM-2 of VC-12 in Atlantic anti-submarine camouflage enters the landing pattern of USS CORE (CVE-13) on 12 April 1944, with flaps, tail hook and landing gear all down. (National Archives/D. Lucabaugh)

An FM-2 of VC-14 taxies forward after landing on USS HOGGATT BAY (CVE-75). The Wildcat is painted in the three color camouflage scheme of Non-specular Sea Blue upper surfaces, Non-specular Intermediate Blue fuselage sides and tail over Non-specular Insignia White undersurfaces. The name 'Judy' has been painted on the cowling in White. (National Archives /D. Lucabaugh)

The pilot of this VC-14 FM-2 turns the aircraft over to the plane captain as the deck crew work to disengage the Wildcat from the crash barrier aboard USS HOGGATT BAY (CVE-75) on 8 October 1944. The Wildcat carries an unusual marking for a Navy aircraft on the cowling, a scantily clad female figure with the name *The Reluctant Maid* above it. (National Archives/J/Dresser)

Radio Mast And Aerials

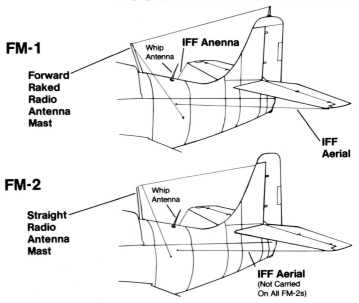

FM-1

Whip Antenna

IFF Anenna

Forward Raked Radio Antenna Mast

IFF Aerial

FM-2

Whip Antenna

Straight Radio Antenna Mast

IFF Aerial (Not Carried On All FM-2s)

A pair of FM-2s of VC-4 return to USS WHITE PLAINS (CVE-66) after completing a combat air patrol on 24 June 1944. The individual aircraft number is carried in Black in the center of the White triangle on the tail and is repeated in White on the cowl ring. (National Archives)

Deck crewmen fold the wings on this FM-2 of VC-85 before the aircraft taxies forward into its assigned parking spot on the bow of USS HOGGATT BAY (CVE-75) on 2 July 1945. A White chevron on the tail was the squadron marking for VC-85 while the double White lightning bolts on the Wildcats in the background identify them as belonging to VC-88. (National Archives)

An overall Glossy Sea Blue FM-2 of VC-93 is chocked and tied down aboard USS PETROF BAY (CVE-80) on 11 May 1945. The four leaf clovers painted on the tail and starboard wing tip and individual aircraft number are in White.(National Archives)

An overall Glossy Sea Blue Marine FM-2 recovers aboard USS SOLOMONS (CVE-67) during carrier qualifications on 3 May 1945. The White cowling ring marks this Wildcat as an advanced trainer. During 1945 USS SOLOMONS was used as a training carrier off the US East Coast. (National Archives/D. Lucabaugh)

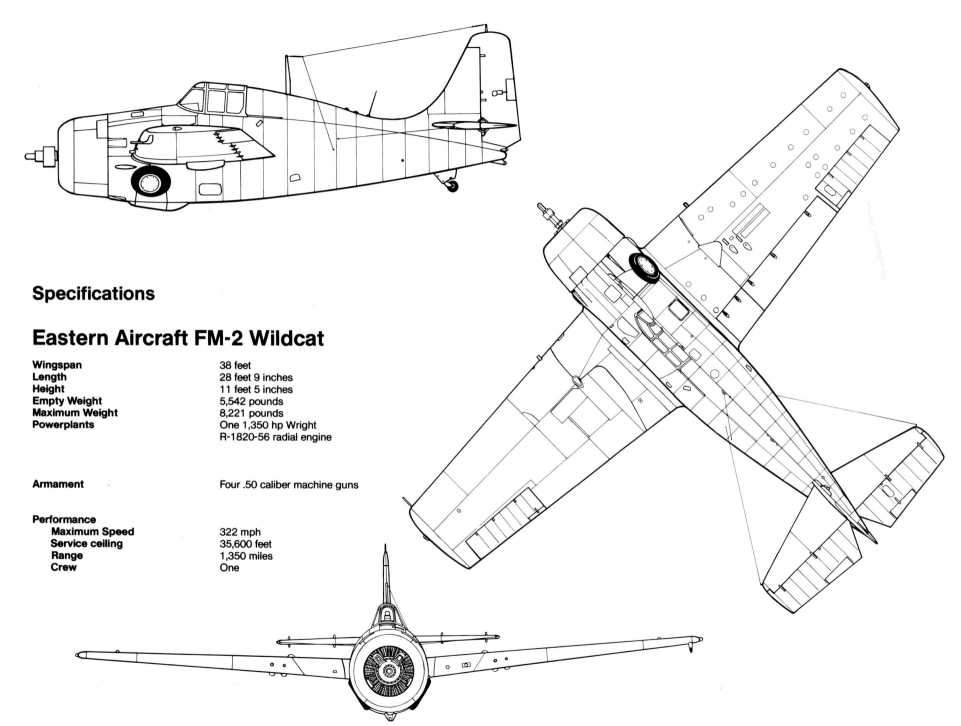

Specifications

Eastern Aircraft FM-2 Wildcat

Wingspan	38 feet
Length	28 feet 9 inches
Height	11 feet 5 inches
Empty Weight	5,542 pounds
Maximum Weight	8,221 pounds
Powerplants	One 1,350 hp Wright R-1820-56 radial engine
Armament	Four .50 caliber machine guns

Performance

Maximum Speed	322 mph
Service ceiling	35,600 feet
Range	1,350 miles
Crew	One

(Above) The taxi director (center below the Wildcat's nose) directs an FM-2 of VC-99 to taxi forward on USS HOGGATT BAY (CVE-75). The Wildcat has been painted with the White tail and wing identification markings assigned to aircraft operating from HOGGATT BAY after 2 June 1945. (National Archives/D. Lucabaugh)

Sack Time, an FM-2 of VC-20, narrowly missed going into the crash barrier on USS KANDASHAN BAY (CVE-76). The ships fire fighters in asbestos suits had moved in on the Wildcat when it appeared that it would hit the barrier. The personal marking, *Sack Time*, is believed to be Yellow. (National Archives)

LTJG McElroy broke the tail wheel of his FM-2 of VC-83 landing aboard USS SARGENT BAY (CVE-83) and went into the barrier on 1 May 1945. A crewman with a CO_2 fire bottle runs to the Wildcat to prevent any spilled fuel from starting a deck fire. (National Archives)

A rocket armed FM-2 of VC-8 takes off from USS MAKIN ISLAND (CVE-93) for an air support mission on 29 March 1945. Late production FM-2s were fitted with three Mk 5 launcher stubs for 5 inch high velocity aircraft rockets (HVAR) under each wing. (National Archives/J. Dresser)

This FM-2 of VC-96 nosed over after engaging the crash barrier aboard USS RUDYERD BAY (CVE-81) following a 1 April 1945 strike against targets on Okinawa. The drop tank is in White, a holdover from the earlier three color camouflage scheme that featured White under-surfaces. (USN/D. Lucabaugh)

An overall Orange-Yellow FM-2 trainer parked on the ramp at the Naval Air Modification Unit (NAMU) Johnsville, Pennsylvania on 9 September 1946. NAMU Johnsville was responsible for training Navy mechanics and had a number of different aircraft types assigned. (NASM)

Mk 5 HVAR Rocket Launchers

FM-2
(Last 1,400 Aircraft Built)

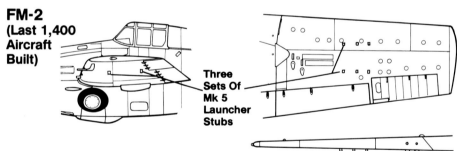

Three Sets Of Mk 5 Launcher Stubs

Mk-5 Zero Length Rocket Launcher Stubs

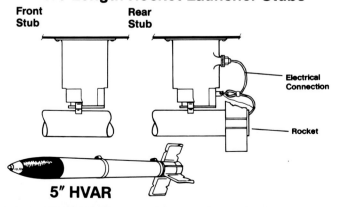

Front Stub

Rear Stub

Electrical Connection

Rocket

5" HVAR

48

Martlet/Wildcat VI

In March of 1944 the British changed the names of all American made aircraft in service. This decision was made to avoid unnecessary confusion between like aircraft types when operating with American forces. F4Fs in British service were assigned the name Wildcat along with the original Martlet mark number. The Martlet I therefore became the Wildcat I, Martlet II was changed to Wildcat II, etc.

During early 1944 the British began receiving the first of an allotment of 370 Eastern Aircraft FM-2s under the designation Wildcat Mk VI. The first squadron to re-equip with the Wildcat VI, No. 881 Squadron aboard HMS PURSUER, became operational on 4 July 1944. The Wildcat Mk VI was identical to the US Navy's FM-2 and was the last of the Martlet/Wildcat series to be delivered to the Royal Navy.

Wildcat Mk VIs served primarily in the Far Eastern Theater of Operations, however, a number of Atlantic based squadrons also re-equipped with the Mk VI. These squadrons took part in attacks against German U-boat bases along the Norwegian coast, anti-shipping operations in the North Atlantic, and supported US Army troops during the Allied invasion of southern France in August of 1944. The last British Wildcat combat victory was on 26 March 1945, during a fighter sweep over northern Norway. Four Wildcat Mk VIs of No 882 Squadron were attacked by a number of Messerschmitt Bf 109s of III/JG-5. One of the Wildcats was damaged in the attack, however, the others were able to shoot down four of the attacking Bf 109s.

Royal Navy Martlet/Wildcats are credited with fifty-three enemy aircraft destroyed in aerial combat; thirty-eight German, eight Italian, six Vichy French, and one Japanese. British records indicate that ten Martlet/Wildcats were lost in aerial combat, giving the Wildcat a 5.3 to 1 victory to loss ratio, which compares favorably with the US Navy/Marine Corps ratio of 6.9 to 1.

Wildcats, both in British and US service, made a significant contribution to the final Allied victory in the Second World War. In the Atlantic US Navy and British Wildcats helped keep the vital shipping lanes open and free of prowling German U-boats. In the Pacific, Wildcats were the mounts of a string of US Marine Corps aces at Guadalcanal, men such as MAJ Joseph Foss, MAJ Marion Carl, MAJ John Smith and LT James Sweet, who are legends in Marine Corps history. A total of eight Wildcat pilots earned the highest award the American people can bestow, the Congressional Medal of Honor, a fitting tribute to the Wildcat and the men who flew her.

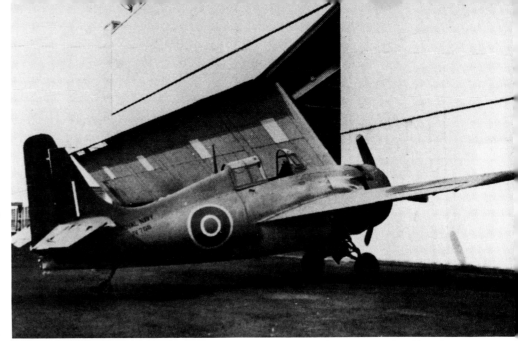

An early production Wildcat Mk VI (JV708) on the Eastern Aircraft ramp at Linden, New Jersey. The Royal Navy received a total of 370 Wildcat Mk VIs under Lend-lease. The first squadron to re-equip with the MK VI was No 881 Squadron aboard HMS PURSUER.

A Wildcat Mk VI (JV752) on a test flight prior to delivery to the Fleet Air Arm. In March of 1944 the British changed the names of all American made aircraft in service to avoid confusion when operating with American forces. Martlets were assigned the name Wildcat along with the Martlet Mark number. Only a few Martlet VIs were delivered before the name change went into effect.

The Wildcat VI was externally identical to the US Navy FM-2 Wildcat and was the last of the Martlet/Wildcat series to be delivered to the British. When the war ended, Wildcats squadrons were quickly disbanded and large numbers of Wildcats were jettisoned at sea.

49

WWII NAVY CARRIER AIR POWER
"in action"
from Squadron/Signal

1081

1036

1029

1079

1064

1082

1054

 **squadron/signal publications, inc.**